TRIUMPH OVER THE IMPOSSIBLE

PAN PARAG
"LEGACY SINCE 1973"

Smart BUDGET
DISH WASH BAR

KOTHARI
GROUP

YES
Packaged Drinking Water

KOTHARI
PRODUCTS PVT. LTD.

SMK
Charitable Trust

EDUCATION

KOTHARI INTERNATIONAL SCHOOL — PUNE

Indrayu Academy of Performing Arts

Our Passion · Their Future KOTHARI STARZ — MUMBAI

Our Passion · Their Future KOTHARI STARZ — PUNE

Our Passion · Their Future KOTHARI STARZ — NOIDA

MANSUKHBHAI KOTHARI NATIONAL SCHOOL — PUNE

KOTHARI INTERNATIONAL SCHOOL — NOIDA

OTHERS
Hospitality
Agriculture
Real Estate
Import Export
We-कल्प
A SENIOR CITIZEN FORUM

Dedicated to the memory of my beloved mother,
Sharda Ben, who we fondly called Baa.

Baa and Babuji

सतीश महाना
अध्यक्ष
उ0 प्र0 विधान सभा

पत्र संख्या :–भृ.भा.अ0वि0स0/2023 दिनांक : 07/06/23
विधान भवन, लखनऊ
फोन नं. : 0522–2238161 (कार्या0)

:: शुभकामना ::

मुझे यह जानकर अति प्रसन्नता हुई कि कोठारी समूह अपना "स्वर्ण जयन्ती" वर्ष मनाने के साथ ही बाबू जी 'मनसुखलाल महादेवभाई कोठारी' की जीवन यात्रा पर आधारित एक पुस्तक का विमोचन करने जा रहा है।

बाबू जी मनसुखलाल महादेवभाई कोठारी सच्चे कर्मयोगी थे। उनका व्यक्तित्व ऐसा था जिसमें मानवता के संस्कार और व्यापार के गुण समान मात्रा में थे। किसी व्यापारिक लक्ष्य के लिए उन्होंने अपने मूल्यों से कभी समझौता नहीं किया, उनकी जीवनी न मात्र वर्तमान पीढ़ी के उद्यमियों, अपितु आने वाली पीढ़ियों को भी प्रेरणा देती रहेगी।

'शून्य से गगन' पुस्तक के लेखक ने बाबू जी मनसुखलाल महादेवभाई कोठारी की जीवन यात्रा को सराहनीय रूप से लिपिबद्ध किया है जिसके लिए वे साधुवाद के पात्र हैं। यह पुस्तक निश्चित रूप से प्रेरणादायक व पठनीय है।

मै उक्त 'पुस्तक' के सफल प्रकाशन हेतु अपनी हार्दिक शुभकामनाएं प्रेषित करता हूँ।

(सतीश महाना)

श्री दीपक कोठारी
चेयरमैन,
कोठारी समूह, 24/19 द मॉल,
कानपुर–208001

Carrying forward a glorious legacy:
Deepak Kothari, son of Mansukh Bhai.

TRIUMPH OVER THE IMPOSSIBLE

Dreams Make the Way

MANSUKH BHAI KOTHARI

Deepak Kothari

MANJUL

Manjul Publishing House

First published in India by

MANJUL

Manjul Publishing House
• C-16, Sector 3, Noida, Uttar Pradesh 201301, India
Website: www.manjulindia.com
Registered Office:
• 2nd Floor, Usha Preet Complex, 42 Malviya Nagar, Bhopal 462 003 – India
Distribution Centres:
Ahmedabad, Bengaluru, Bhopal, Kolkata, Chennai,
Hyderabad, Mumbai, New Delhi, Pune

Triumph Over The Impossible: Dreams Make the Way – Mansukh Bhai Kothari
by Deepak Kothari

This edition first published in 2024

ISBN 978-93-5543-583-5

Printed and bound in India by Thomson Press (India) Ltd.

CONTENTS

SECTION – 3

Preface

The life history of Mansukh Bhai Mahadev Bhai Kothari, the founder of the *Pan Parag Group,* is not a simple journey of rags to riches by mere hard work and luck but a beacon of chasing one's dream with a clear mindset of success. Notwithstanding obstacles, scarcity, and poverty with no financial support or otherwise, he built his fortune by sheer dint of conviction, beliefs, and self-confidence. Every fall on his way to success was always a fall forward, and he took every incidence, setback, obstacle, and challenge as a lesson to grow and rise.

Imagine a youth from a very ordinary family background who hails from a remote village, Narali, in Gujarat. At the tender age of eighteen, he travels to Kanpur, a faraway city, with only fourteen rupees in his pocket but a dream to become rich to support his family of five brothers, two sisters, and parents. But his enthusiasm, zeal, passion, and untiring attitude motivated him to prove himself, and in just three decades, he scripted an unbelievable success story in independent India.

His memory was like wet cement. Whatever came his way since childhood made an everlasting impression on his mind and heart. He learned his profession's hard work and honesty from his father, Mahadev Bhai Kothari, who had a small grocery shop in his native village. The dignity of labour and the value of money were his first lessons from his father, as well as family values and *sanskar* from his mother, Maniben Kothari. His parents taught him every aspect of life. Along with business principles, they also instilled in him the values of humanity and kindness and always encouraged him to progress. This inspiration remained his guiding light throughout life.

It's inspiring to think of and visualize the impossible feat of success by a man who started his professional career without any support except his will power, hard work, and visionary approach.

When it comes to capturing the life journey of such a towering personality and weaving the different shades of his journey into a single book, it's inspiring, challenging, and, at the same time, a social responsibility to show millions of people that fortune and success depend not on your financial or social status but on your self-belief and passion.

Biography is always very close to the factual history of a person's journey, especially if it is taken up as a task by none other than the son, who witnessed and knew each and every fact of his life either on his own or through his mother or family. His son, Deepak Kothari, has taken this filial responsibility to show the world how the impossible can be converted into hope and possibilities.

Widely known in the business world as Babuji, Mansukh Bhai started a simple cottage industry from home, making it a 'Brand' through his unwavering perseverance and dedication. In addition to making numerous people self-reliant, he provided a new direction to society. The extraordinary journey of *Pan Parag* was a testament to his determination to make a dream come true. Even today, it may seem impossible to achieve what he did, but all challenges and obstacles collapsed in front of Mansukh Bhai's dedication, never-say-die attitude, and dream of reaching the pinnacle of success. Amidst the storms of business, he kept moving toward his goal and made *Pan Parag* synonymous with *pan masala.*

Success is attainable through firm determination and passion.

Mansukh Bhai held firm faith in his heart that his success would be acknowledged one day. He tirelessly ventured into one business after another, always persistent in his passion and courage to move ahead.

This book is not about the growth of a product or business but rather about a person's passion, confidence, and struggle. It teaches us that a person's strength is reflected in their ability to fall and stand up again with renewed energy.

Mansukh Bhai used to enthusiastically share his memories, life journey, and saga of struggle with his loved ones. This book brings his memories back to life from those moments.

Obstacles and roadblocks are no match for individuals like Mansukh Bhai. Their determination and positivity guarantee their success as they fearlessly pursue their dreams and aspirations. This portrayal of Mansukh Bhai's life is a sincere effort to encapsulate his remarkable journey, unshakeable self-assurance, and deep dedication to principles, values, and the betterment of humanity.

The biography includes dialogues based on Babuji's memories, vividly brought to life through Deepak Kothari's rich recollections and experiences. I take immense pride in associating with him and translating his emotions and storytelling into this book. I am confident that readers will find this portrayal genuinely captivating.

– From the Co-author's Desk

Sweat and Blood, But No Tears

By the time I turned fourteen, my father, Mansukh Bhai Kothari, fondly called Babuji, had already established himself as a successful businessman. We were three siblings, being brought up in comfort with all possible facilities. When you reach this age of adolescence, you want to explore the world beyond your family and learn what exists beyond school, hometown, or country. I was no exception to this universal rule. I started reading motivational stories with great interest. Teachers in school imparted the message of moving forward in life with uncompromising integrity and relentless hard work. Babuji too emphasized the same values.

In our lives, we all know, our father is always a vital pillar of support and a quintessential role model. His life journey always serves as a wellspring of inspiration. During my teenage years, I observed my father's remarkable confidence, understanding, and passion through his body language and gait. Even at that age, my intuition told me that Babuji's personality was unique, but little did I know about his tremendous journey of struggle between 1943 and 1950. Babuji was a person who achieved great success on a regular basis. Yet, he always remained humble and grounded in his approach towards life. He never boasted about his outstanding achievements. He firmly believed that you shouldn't allow your ego to empower you; instead, learn to tame it, and your life will be wonderful.

Growing up, we had some idea of the struggle of life from the hushed conversations between our parents, but we had absolutely no sense of its depth. When we started understanding the world around us, we became curious to know Babuji's early struggle, but he would often change the subject. Perhaps Babuji's thought behind this was that knowing about his arduous initial struggle could hurt his children's tender minds or our self-confidence could waver. But finally, one day, he agreed to our repeated requests. That day, the things that Babuji shared in detail about his journey from village life to the business world not only amazed us but left us awestruck too. Everything was unthinkable to us.

Imagine the social, political, and economic milieu eight decades ago. The era of colonialism... atrocities by the British... shameless plunder of India's resources... poverty, hunger, and unemployment all around... Amidst such a frightening scenario, an eighteen-year-old youth resolves to break these shackles. With just a small amount in his pocket, he travels almost one thousand kilometres from the comfort of his home. His only dream is to bring smiles to his parents' faces. This young man makes three cities earlier unknown to him his *karmasthali* (workplace). And in just three decades, he establishes a business empire with extraordinary passion and unwavering determination to move forward tirelessly. Doesn't it seem like a magical story? Yes, it sounds like that, but this is the incredible story of my father's struggle.

After becoming one of the top business personalities in the country with the *Pan Parag* brand, many anecdotes of Babuji's success story were prominently published in the media from time to time. His fantastic success had become an unsolved mystery for the masses. Many professional writers wanted to script his biography. They approached Babuji and tried their best to convince him, but as a humble person, he always avoided the limelight. He used to say a big no to any such proposal in a polite way. His simple response was:

"Don't make me great. The values of my parents and the hard work of my life partner have equally contributed to my success."

It has been almost nine years since Babuji set out on his eternal journey, but his ideals and values inspire us every moment. During this time, I came to the idea of bringing the extraordinary life story of a multifaceted personality like him before the people, but it was a difficult challenge to accurately portray Babuji's charismatic personality and incredible success. If you are an avid book reader, you would know that bookshelves worldwide are filled with books on success stories. Most of these books have similar, often repeated words, but specific success stories are unmatched in their respective fields. They have their own category, sparkling like stars. The success story of Babuji is unique and stands in a category of its own.

It is equally important to highlight another significant difference between today's achievements and the great success others achieved decades ago. In today's era, billion-dollar industries have been established worldwide in the form of business gurus and personality development gurus. With financial agencies providing loans to start businesses or pursue higher education, Millennials and Gen Z have an added advantage. But think of those who scaled great heights of success without all these facilities. It's like conducting oil exploration in the desert without drilling equipment or removing mountain-like hurdles with only a hammer. But Mansukh Bhai, the founder of *Pan parag,* did exactly that. The young generation can learn a lot by reading Babuji's life story because I firmly believe that although things and technologies have undergone a sea change and challenges are different, the fundamental mantras of success are still the same.

Mansukh Bhai was a tremendous visionary in business. His innovative and sharp mind was always full of new ideas. He understood the market's pulse closely; hence, success touched his feet. He was an advertising guru in his own way. He was far ahead of his time. Iconic advertisements like *Baraatiyon Ka Swagat Pan Parag Se Kijiye* and *Dhoom Macha De, Rang Jama De* were the products of his creative mind, and he also convinced the shining film stars of that era to act in them. His kind and caring relationship with the company's employees was a prime example of effective human resource management. He took his cottage industry to the top of the success ladder. In this sense, he was also a true pioneer of startups. He had already worked on Corporate Social Responsibility (CSR) long before others conceived it. He also understood the importance of women's empowerment in the fifties itself.

It is a matter of great pride for me that I was not only a witness to Babuji's remarkable life journey but also became an integral part of it later. I feel blessed to carry forward his rich legacy. While struggling hard, Babuji sent letters and telegrams to his parents as there was no speed communication in those days. The collection of these letters and telegrams is like priceless treasures I have safely preserved. The conversations between family members on various occasions are still fresh in my mind. I had heard about some from Babuji, while in some others, I was also a participant. We have included these dialogues in the book in a lively manner to preserve the fragrance of the story.

In the end, I would like to express deep gratitude to my better half, *Arti Kothari,* and my close friend, *Mr Pradeep Srivastava,* who not only encouraged me but also took a keen interest in the entire writing process of the biography, so that every important aspect of Babuji's life was included in it.

I am also thankful to my younger brother, a family friend, *Mr Vikas Chaturvedi (Chunna Bhaiya),* and my business partner, Late *Mr Lakshmi Narayan Mehrotra (Lalla Bhaiya),* who guided me in every challenging phase of life. For this, I will always be indebted. This gratitude section can only be completed by mentioning the name of Dr Avinash Gupta. He is my childhood friend; even Babuji loved him as his son. Because of this great bonding, he is known as the adopted son of Babuji. As a business consultant, he fulfilled Babuji's dream of starting a school. I extend my great appreciation for making it possible. My heartfelt gratitude goes to *Dr Om Shankar Gupta* and *my Chief Secretary, Dr Amit Singh,* who captured my emotions in the best possible manner and weaved them into beautiful words.

My grandson, Indrayu Kothari, deserves special thanks for providing his valuable inputs to ensure the perfection of the presentation. His idea to bring about transcreation rather than a literal translation of the original work (Shunya Se Gagan) made all the difference. He has proved that he is an equally gifted great-grandson of Babuji.

Mansukh Bhai possessed numerous exceptional qualities that are difficult to list exhaustively. He believed that constantly shifting goals, even after achieving success, keeps the flag of victory flying high. This book is a biography and an authentic document of a true *karmayogi's* unbelievable life journey. To reflect my genuine emotions, I have modified the famous idiom 'blood, sweat, and tears' into 'blood, sweat, but no tears, as Babuji never cursed his modest background. Instead, through sheer hard work, he crafted his own destiny.

In Babuji's words, the world remembers only those who do something different from the worn-out track or write something different, which people can read and get inspiration from in the future. So dear readers, enjoy reading and see how much you can learn from it.

– DEEPAK KOTHARI

Chairman and *Managing Director, Kothari Group*

Babuji Was a Unique Combination of Discipline and Affection

Expressing Babuji's exceptional personality traits can be challenging, but he was undoubtedly a gem in the business world and an outstanding leader. His story of struggle is more powerful than any inspirational tale, as he fought like a true warrior in pursuit of his goals. Babuji firmly believed in the importance of maintaining strong relationships and never wavered in his dedication to both family and business commitments. Every memory of Babuji is unforgettable, and the book on his life is a testament to his greatness.

I am incredibly fortunate to have the opportunity to share my experiences with Babuji, in this book. When I first entered my in-laws' house on 27 May 1975, after my wedding, I had heard about Babuji's overbearing personality and loud voice. Initially, I perceived him to be strict, but soon, I realized that he had a unique combination of discipline and affection - a rare quality in people. To me, he was not merely a father-in-law but a loving father who always treated me as his daughter. He showered me with so much love and care that it is impossible to express it in words.

Although associated with the male-dominated social system of the past, I am proud to say that Babuji pioneered women's empowerment. He made *Baa* his partner in business and encouraged me to leave the kitchen and learn about the intricacies of the company in the factory. Under his guidance, I gained a close understanding of the production and packaging processes and learned a lot. Thanks to his inspiration and blessings, I am now able to manage and run all the schools of Kothari Group successfully. For this, I consider myself truly blessed.

Babuji's remarkable principles and exclusive management style have been our guiding light, illuminating our path and leading us towards further success. Your blessings have been a constant source of hope and inspiration, and we hope they will continue to remain with us wherever you are.

My utmost respect and gratitude to you, Babuji.

– Arti Deepak Kothari

My ideal, my Dada…

People associate him with a larger-than-life picture. In my eyes, my dada was a humble human who has faced life at its worst but was still always a happy and positive mindset person. Even in the worst situations, he has always viewed life in a beautiful way.

He loved interesting and knowledgeable company, his will for learning new things…always impressed me. The biggest learning I can say I have got from him is being in the present.

He had a knack…which has directly transferred itself to me… we always view difficulty as a chance to jump to bigger achievements… I learned from him to take things from people (except advice), which we both have patience for. We both had an equal silent take on life… the best quality in dada was his humility…which I have experienced through so many of our holidays and work trips.

There is a famous proverb… *"An empire lasts for only two generations…"* I can hope and contradict that ours is an empire in not the third but the fourth generation (Indrayu, you better keep it up) of humility and attaining the highest goal in a silent mode.

– Mitesh Kothari
(Grandson)

Dada… An epitome of strength and perseverance.

When I first met him, I found it very interesting that he kept asking me way too many questions, seeing the curve of my feet, as he believed that it reflects Goddess Laxmi blessing the house. He was definitely very superstitious, he used to call me for any silly reason before he left home in the morning for office. Initially, I used to keep a bindi on my palm (Baa had told me to) and put it on when he left. He used to never step out without eating a spoon of masala and a sip of water…

If I look back now… one instance I can never forget about him – a strong person like him (battling Parkinson's Disease)…he refused to get on the wheelchair…then one morning, I told dada 'Indrayu is in his pram... you can be in wheelchair and you both can do a walk together in mornings' …he tried it out, and finally it all came through. Baa was so relieved.

Many such incidents, very small for others but a battle for a strong man…people only identify super humans like him as industrious, successful strong characters…to me what I see of him as strength was his ability to change and adapt with time and generations…his ability stay strong despite failing health…his will for a life without negativity…being absolutely grounded…yet living life and every waking day to the fullest.

Dada was all that he was because he had a wife like Baa …that is unquestionably true in their case.

– Urvi Kothari
(Daughter-in-law)

I have very fond memories of my Bade Dada…

He was a very affectionate person and always taught me the importance of discipline and time management.

During the days when he was in a wheelchair, I used to take him out and during that time, he used to tell me lots of things, such as how to spend family time and how to concentrate when you're at work.

I have learnt a lot of good things from him. One common feature we share is that he was fond of parties and get-togethers with his friends and dear ones and I too love it.

Salute to you, my bade dada, I miss you...

– Indrayu Kothari,
Great Grandson
Son of Mitesh and Urvi Kothari

"A grandfather is someone with silver in his hair and gold in his heart."

This is how my grandfather was. I have tons of memories with him – happy, sad, loving, argumentative, but still he was the one who was the leader and knew how to raise his family.

I haven't yet come across a similar personality. His vision was far superior to other people's. I guess our grandparents were more like friends than parents as we used to play cards, talk about various stuff, go on holidays etc... I can't forget them ever in my life and still feel their presence and blessings with us. Now I really feel that *"Grandfathers are antique little boys."*

– Hemani Gowani
(Granddaughter)

Every generation revolts against its fathers and makes friends with its grandfathers.

Thanks to Hemani, I got the opportunity to share holidays and my time in Delhi with an inspiring and loving grandfather-in-law, who has always been a legend of new ideas and hardworking.

– Vinod Gowani
(Grandson-in-law)

Dada is an icon in my mind. He was and always will be the force that kept the entire family together. He was admirable, someone who built himself with each experience he had.

Dada passed away a few years ago and I still think about him every single day – the impact Dada and Baa had in my life is profound, one that I haven't been able to extract from any other member in my life. The energy he brought into every conversation and the way he patiently heard us out.

The last time we met was when we visited Ahmedabad for his birthday and I'm so glad we were able to celebrate with him and the people he loved most.

Dada and Baa, you will always be the greatest inspiration for all of us and we are deeply grateful to be able to carry your name and legacy forward.

– Kavya
Great Granddaughter
(Daughter of Hemani and Vinod Gowani)

My great-grand-pa passed away when I was only 9 years old. That was 8 years ago but I feel like the day we met was yesterday. We were in Ahmedabad celebrating his 90th birthday and I cannot forget the joy on his face. He was full of life even 4 months before his eventual passing away. My 'Bade Nanu' was always really joyous and that's what I will take away from his life.

– Krishraj
Great Grandson
(Son of Hemani and Vinod Gowani)

Special Acknowledgements

The invaluable support and emotional aid that late *Shri Omkar Nath Chaturvedi* provided during challenging times will forever remain etched in my heart. His contribution to the success of *Pan Parag* cannot be overstated. Babuji's vision was made a reality with the help of Shri Chaturvedi, who was an integral part of the journey. I remember him with utmost respect and gratitude for his unwavering support and contributions that helped shape the company's future.

I am filled with immense gratitude for late *Shri Ramji Mehrotra.* His tireless equal efforts to present the incredible life journey of Babuji to the new generation have given us a chance to pass on an inspiring legacy. Shri Ramji was not just our business advisor but a valuable member of our family who shared our vision of bringing about positive change. He was a true friend, brother, and mentor who guided me at every step, and his contributions were priceless. His memory will forever inspire us to continue making a difference. I am grateful for the wisdom and support he shared, which made all the difference in my journey. Shri Ramji Mehrotra was remarkable, and I am honoured to have had him in my life.

YES
सेवन अप
OK
PAN PARAG
PAN MASALA

Sunset of an Era: The Last Journey of a True *Karmayogi*

Great men never die, and it is up to us to keep
them immortal by continuing
the work they have commenced.

– Mahatma Gandhi (Harijan, 1947)

On 27 November 2015, it was around 2 o'clock after midnight when Deepak Bhai's phone unexpectedly rang. Deepak Bhai had just finished a busy day and was fast asleep. However, the ringing phone startled him awake, causing him to quickly reach over and answer it. The call was from his mother, *Baa.*

Baa called out, her voice filled with pain, "Deepak...Deepak...?" Deepak Bhai, slightly nervous, responded, "Yes, Baa, please tell me, what happened?" Baa replied, "Your father isn't saying anything." Deepak Bhai suddenly couldn't understand the whole situation.

Deepak Bhai hurried to his father's room, still wearing his nightclothes. It didn't take him long to get there, but when he arrived, he saw his mother standing by his father's bedside, gazing at him. He felt anxious and uncertain about what was happening as he approached them.

Deepak called out to his father, "Papa, Papa!" But when there was no response, he suddenly became nervous and apprehensive. He checked his father's pulse and then rushed to the phone to call the family doctor. Within ten minutes, the doctor arrived, and Deepak shared his concerns. The doctor tried to calm him down and began the checkup. Suddenly, the doctor stopped and covered Mansukh Bhai with a sheet. Without saying a word, he got up and announced, "He is no more."

When Baa heard what the doctor said, darkness clouded her vision. Deepak Bhai was in disbelief and almost screamed, "What? Doctor, please check again, please!" Amid the chaos, Baa fainted and fell unconscious. Deepak Bhai was frantic and ran to his mother's side, forgetting his anguish. The doctor tried to revive her, and after some time, Baa regained consciousness. She started crying while looking at her husband's head in her lap. Arti, Deepak Bhai's wife, who had followed him to Babuji's room, immediately understood the gravity of the situation. She cared for Baa while everyone was trying to cope with the shock.

On the other hand, the doctor picked up his bag without giving any reaction and walked outside. Deepak Bhai was utterly stunned and speechless. He could not understand how this happened so suddenly, but he was facing the eternal truth of life. His father, Mansukh Bhai, had passed away.

After some time, Deepak Bhai regained control of his emotions. He then called his sister, Rita, who lived in America. After the phone rang several times, Rita answered but didn't speak. Before she could say anything, Deepak spoke in an emotion-choked voice: "Ri...Rita..."

Rita received several phone calls from Deepak Bhai. However, he was unable to speak clearly as his throat was choked. This made Rita anxious and caused her heart rate to increase. After a few minutes, Deepak Bhai could speak with incredible difficulty.

His words seemed like glass to Rita's ears, causing emotional devastation.

Deepak Bhai was inconsolable as he spoke to Rita on the phone. With a heavy heart, he shared the news of Babuji's passing. "I had brought him to Kanpur hoping to give him the best care, but he left us silently. I couldn't even provide him with the care he deserved," he said, his voice breaking with emotion.

Afterward, Deepak Bhai informed his elder brother Vikram Kothari, who was out of the city for work, about the news on the phone. He then shared the news with his son Mitesh Kothari, daughter Hemani, daughter-in-law Urvi, and grandson Indrayu, who were all in Mumbai. After that, he informed close friends and other relatives of the family one by one about Babuji's demise.

People rushed to his room when they heard about Mansukh Bhai's death. Aarti, Deepak Bhai's wife, cared for Baa while also trying to console her husband. But despite her best efforts, Deepak Bhai could not control his tears while Baa's sobs echoed through the silent night. Everyone present was gripped by an overwhelming sense of sadness, and no one knew what to say.

The news of Mansukh Bhai's passing spread like wildfire through Kanpur, and the outpouring of support was heart-touching. One could see a constant stream of people coming to his residence, Sukhdham. After considering everyone's opinion, the family unanimously decided to keep Mansukh Bhai's mortal remains at Sukhdham for two days, allowing everyone to have a chance to pay last respects to their beloved Babuji. Even though Rita, Mansukh Bhai's daughter, was in America, and his elder son and close relatives were away from Kanpur city, the family welcomed anyone who wished to have a final darshan of Babuji and be with them during this time of mourning.

Over two days, fans of Babuji from across India and beyond visited Sukhdham to pay their respects to the courageous warrior of Karmpath. On 29 November, his final journey from Sukhdham to Bhairav Ghat began, and the entire city came to a standstill as a massive crowd gathered to bid him farewell. From his residence in Tilak Nagar to Bhairav Ghat, heads could be seen as far as the eye could see. It seemed like the entire city was mourning his loss. Advertisers of Pan Parag spontaneously put up hoardings throughout Kanpur as a tribute to Babuji without explicit instructions or orders. This was a heartfelt outpouring of grief and respect for the departed soul.

The city of Kanpur paid tribute to an exceptional individual who served as a shining example of hard work. He decorated his entire life with relentless hard work and dedication, helping countless people live with dignity and respect. He was loved by everyone, and his departure left an irreplaceable void in the hearts of the city's inhabitants.

Grief is like the ocean, with its ebbing and flowing waves, sometimes calm and sometimes violent. In moments of mourning, we must learn to keep swimming, as someone once said. The family, close friends, and numerous fans of Mansukh Bhai were slowly coming to terms with the painful reality that their beloved Babuji was no longer with them in this world.

Two years ago, he embraced his roots once again!

Let's discover the beauty and depth of a heart-touching poem by Harivansh Rai Bachchan.

Neelam -se pallav tut gaye,

Markat- se sathi chhut gaye,

Atke phir bhi do peet paat

Jeevan-daali ko tham, sakhe!

Hai yeah patjhad ki sham, sakhe!

(Just like this gem, sapphire, the fallen leaves were delicate and soft. The comrades departed, leaving the emerald behind. Who pondered the cause in the fading eve? As the emerald loses its lustre, it doesn't polish, but fractures. In its final phase, the leaf turns yellow. Yet, in a glimmer of hope, it clings to the branch and twig. Even in the autumn's embrace. Here, the poet, in a poignant self-address, grapples with his mind, his inner turmoil, and the profound conflict within.)

Babuji longed for the warmth of his homeland and the sense of belonging he had been away from for decades, which made his heart ache. Although this poem captured his emotions, nothing could compare to his longing. Despite his age, Babuji was determined to reconnect with the source of his initial childhood happiness. He knew it was time to return to his homeland and find peace in the embrace of his roots.

In 2013, just two years before his passing, Mansukh Bhai expressed his desire to be closer to his birthplace, to his son Deepak Bhai and daughter-in-law Arti. Despite his serious illnesses, Mansukh Bhai was the head of the household, and his wishes were honoured. As per his request, he was then relocated to Ahmedabad. As Mansukh Bhai, a prominent figure in the Gujarati community, lay there struggling with physical pain, his mind was fully engrossed. Despite his bodily limitations, the constant stream of visitors brought him emotional relief and contentment. The glow on his face was a testament to the positive impact of these interactions, and even Baa, who was present with him, felt a renewed sense of energy. However, as fate would have it, there were further twists in store for Mansukh Bhai's journey.

In December 2014, two loving nephews, Raju Bhai and Nilesh Bhai, contacted Deepak Bhai with concerning news. Their beloved uncle Babuji was in poor health, and his condition was worsening by the day. Despite Baa's unwavering dedication to caring for him, Babuji's health was deteriorating. They implored Deepak Bhai to bring them to Kanpur, where they believed Babuji's condition would improve. Raju Bhai and Nilesh Bhai's heartfelt plea was rooted in their deep concern for their uncle's well-being and their desire to see him live in comfort and peace.

Deepak Bhai attentively listened to all the details that Raju Bhai and Nilesh Bhai shared with him over the phone. After analyzing the situation, he swiftly decided to bring Baa and Babuji from Ahmedabad to Kanpur. However, the major challenge he faced was that Babuji was unwilling to come to Kanpur. It was an arduous task to convince him, considering his nature. Deepak Bhai knew that his father's health was delicate, so he was determined to find a way to win over his father's stubbornness and bring him to Kanpur.

Medicine was being administered regularly in Ahmedabad, but Babuji's health was continuously deteriorating. Deepak Bhai thought that no matter what happened, he would bring Babuji from Ahmedabad to Kanpur, keep him in front of his eyes, and take care of him. Therefore, he called Baa in Ahmedabad to inform her about his decision. Deepak Bhai spoke with a confident tone, "Baa... Now both of you are coming to Kanpur... I am here... I will look after... Babuji will also like it... and I will also get the satisfaction of staying with him... I am confident it will improve his mood and overall well-being."

Baa said, "Okay, as you think is right… but only if Babuji wants to come…."

Deepak Bhai replied, "No, I will not listen to anything now. I will not accept anything. Babuji has to come to Kanpur..."

After saying this, Deepak Bhai disconnected the call, leaving Baa's response unknown.

Deepak Bhai immediately booked a flight from Kanpur to Ahmedabad. Upon arriving in Ahmedabad, he was heartbroken to see his father's condition. He quickly contacted his friends and arranged for a chartered air ambulance without wasting time. The following day, he and his father were en route back to Kanpur. Throughout the journey, Deepak Bhai kept his father's head in his lap and spoke to him reassuringly, offering comfort during what was undoubtedly a difficult time. When they arrived in Kanpur, they found out that the plane of the then Governor of the state, Ram Naik, was about to take off at Chakeri Airport, which meant that no other planes could land until it had departed. However, Deepak Bhai refused to give up hope. With the help of his friends, he contacted the Air Traffic Control (ATC) and requested an earlier landing for the air ambulance, citing his father's critical health condition. The ATC informed the Governor about the situation, who gave the green signal for the air ambulance bringing Babuji to land first.

The Honourable Governor acted swiftly upon receiving information about the arrival of the renowned industrialist Mansukh Bhai at the airport. Without any delay, the Governor instructed the officers at the airport to assist Mansukh Bhai even before the air ambulance carrying him touched down. As soon as 'Babuji was taken down from the air ambulance, the Governor met him, inquired about his well-being, and wished him a speedy recovery. The devoted son, Deepak Bhai, assisted his father to his room and stayed with him all day, attending to his needs. Throughout the day, people came in large numbers to visit Babuji, including distributors, agency holders, retailers, and his ardent admirers. The crowd had grown significantly by evening, with ordinary and special people flocking to Sukhdham, their residence in Kanpur, to seek blessings from Babuji.

Babuji was of exceptional character and charm, and his mere presence could attract people towards him, regardless of whether they knew him personally or not. Unsurprisingly, news of his stay at Sukhdham spread like wildfire, bringing people from all walks of life to seek his guidance and support. Despite his frailty and limited communication ability, he remained steadfast in his commitment to helping others, a testament to his selflessness and generosity. However, over time, as Mansukh Bhai's treatment continued, and despite the best efforts of Baa, Deepak Bhai, and Aarti, Babuji's health began to worsen, ultimately confining him to his bed. Though he occasionally tried to go to his office with assistance, he always returned home to rest, and his health continued to deteriorate steadily over a year.

The life of Mansukh Bhai was a true testament to perseverance and resilience. Despite facing numerous challenges, he never gave up and persevered through every difficulty. Even in his final days, he refused to burden anyone with his needs and instead embarked on his eternal journey with grace and dignity. Mansukh Bhai may have been ordinary, but his life was nothing short of extraordinary. His compelling journey from humble beginnings to achieving great heights is an undeniable inspiration to us all.

As the adage goes, "*Challenges are like gifts, compelling us to discover new strengths.*" Mansukh Bhai embodied this philosophy throughout his life. He saw every obstacle as an opportunity to grow and learn, and each achievement motivated him to set even higher goals.

Started working at the age of just ten...

Mansukh Bhai's story is truly remarkable and serves as a powerful reminder of the potential within us all. At just ten years of age, he began working alongside his father in their small grocery business, despite minimal earnings. However, this only spurred on his desire to create a better life for himself and his family. With passion and perseverance, he left home at eighteen with a negligible amount in pocket and set out to achieve his goals. Against all odds, Mansukh Bhai's unwavering commitment paid off as he became the proud owner of a vast business empire. His story is a testament to the incredible power of hard work and self-belief, proving that even the *smallest steps taken in the right direction can lead to great success.*

Amazing Businessman with an Unparalleled Personality

"It takes years to build a reputation and
a few minutes to ruin it. If you think about it,
you will definitely do things differently."

– Warren Buffett, One of the Most Successful Investors of All Time

The lines of Pandit Narendra Sharma's poem ask why the Ganga river flows *(Ganga bahati ho kyun)*, but it continues to flow freely, answering every question as it goes. The Ganga springs from a small source and makes a daily journey to meet the ocean. While there are other rivers, the Ganga is unique, representing an idea and a culture. Some consider the Ganga a goddess, but it remains sanctified and uninterrupted regardless of individual beliefs. Mansukh Bhai's life journey was similar to the holy stream of the Ganga, as the journey he began decades ago continues towards its ever changing goalposts, with the next generations carrying the torch. Although the appearance has changed, the ideas and values that Mansukh Bhai adopted have become everlasting traditions.

Mansukh Bhai was an extraordinary individual who excelled as a Karmpath traveller, businessman, and fighter against all odds of life. He never lost hope and kept pushing forward, upholding his family and business traditions while pioneering new startups. Today, his values, ethics, traditions, and product legacy thrive. Whether it's Pan Parag, Yes mineral water, or any other product, all are progressing on the growth path, much like the Ganga river. Furthermore, his products are also adapting to the rapidly changing corporate world. Maintaining success once achieved is challenging, but the next generation is doing a great job following Mansukh Bhai's approach of doing things differently every day to stay ahead.

Mansukh Bhai's wise words remind us that *without the drive and curiosity to work, one can quickly become consumed by one's ego. Unfortunately, this self-absorption prevents individuals from positively contributing to their lives or society. Recognizing the value of hard work and ambition is essential, as these qualities can lead to personal growth and meaningful societal progress.*

Mansukh Bhai started his journey at 18 with just Rs 14 in his pocket. He diligently worked for 30 years and built a thriving business empire from scratch. Despite his remarkable achievements, he never let success go to his head and remained humble. He was a trailblazer in creating and managing homegrown industries, which was considered impossible then. Even after great success, he remained grounded, valued his family, showed gratitude to his loved ones, and always remembered his roots. He received his early education from a village school he held in high regard all his life. Mansukh Bhai was deeply influenced by his mother's teachings of Geeta and Ramayana, which inspired him to lead a dutiful life and follow the path of Karma.

Despite his great success, Mansukh Bhai always remained calm and composed because he knew the story of the tree: the more fruit it bears, the more it bends. He also understood that people forget about wealthy individuals, their wealth, and even kings and princes. People remember those who gave generously, built water kiosks and Dharamshalas, and gave without expecting anything in return. Mansukh Bhai was naturally humble and did not like to be called great. He believed that success in any endeavour requires strong morale, determination, and the willingness to work tirelessly day and night.

He was an exceptional businessman who engaged in various types of businesses throughout his life. However, what made him stand out was his unique approach to financing. He never borrowed money from any source, including banks, moneylenders, or financial institutions. He also never obtained any licenses for his businesses. Despite these unconventional practices, he became a well-known industrialist in the country. His philosophy was simple: "Give cash, take cash means give money and take goods." Mansukh Bhai was stringent when it came to borrowing money. Even after great success, he never lent a single penny to anyone. This was indeed a remarkable aspect of his character.

He was 'special' even amongst the special

Mansukh Bhai was an extraordinary individual who stood out even among the exceptional. He didn't believe in the lines on his palms but instead carved out his path to success through hard work and dedication. He firmly believed that anyone who is committed to his/her duty, exhibits courage, and is ready to work tirelessly can achieve success. Despite having a large number of admirers, Mansukh Bhai had no one to rely on for help. He worked hard and was determined, which helped him achieve wealth and success.

SECTION 1

Good parents give their children roots and wings.
Roots to know where home is, wings to fly away and
exercise what's been taught to them.

— Jonas Edward Salk, American Medical Researcher

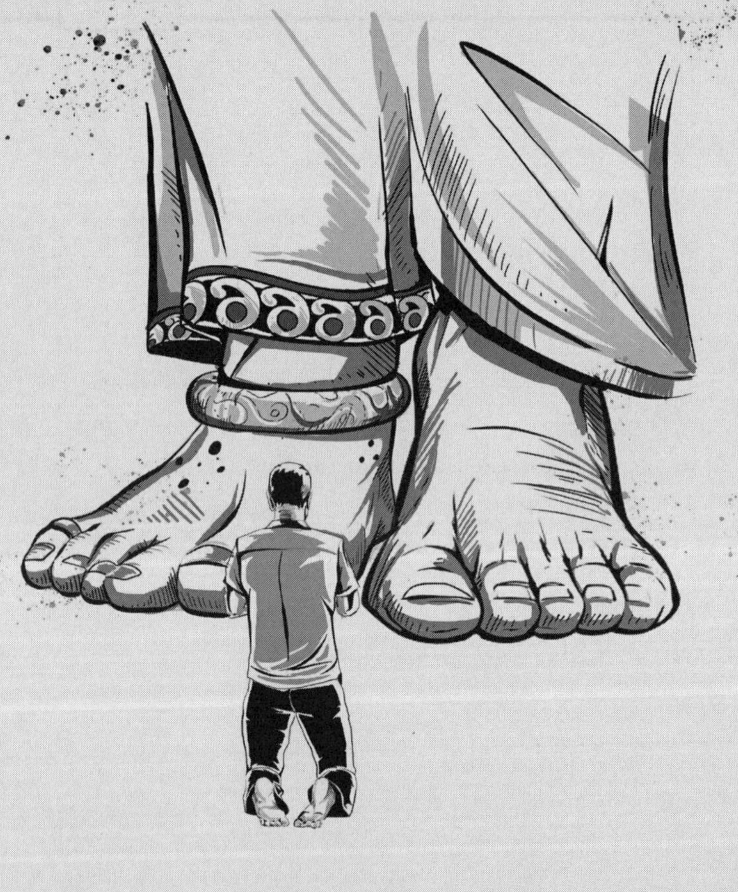

1

Tracing the Roots

"If you were not born with a silver spoon,
take any spoon, and coat it with silver."

—Michael Bassey Johnson,
Night of a Thousand Thoughts

Let us take an imaginary trip to rural India about ninety years ago in 1935 and draw a picture of what the evenings there would have been like... We chose Narali village in Gujarat's Surendranagar district to travel back in time. The evening on the day of our journey is no different. The shadows are getting longer as the sun is about to set on the western horizon of the village. People are returning home after a day's hard work. While the colours of the sunset, orange, red, or pink, look mystical and spread beauty in the atmosphere, on the contrary, there is no trace of happiness, contentment, or dreams of a better future on the faces of the people. The air of despondency and depression piqued our curiosity, prompting us to stay for a week.

After returning from that fanciful stay to the present, we painted a vivid picture of that village scene. That evening, we saw that when a man with a magnetic personality walked forward, almost everyone greeted him. He was Mahadev Bhai, who was very much part of the crowd of villagers. He was trailed by his ten-year-old son, Mansukh, who was walking at a steady pace. Both of them adorned traditional Indian clothing. In addition to that, Mahadev Bhai wore *kilangi* on his turban. He had a very appealing personality and commanded great respect in the village, and his son Mansukh was adored by everyone as well. Mahadev Bhai ran a small grocery shop in the village. His behaviour towards all his customers, was very polite. Even those who borrowed goods were treated with respect by him. Until that time, there was no electricity in the village. He used to open his shop even in the light of lanterns, so that tired people returning from work could buy the goods they needed. But for some reason, he had closed his shop early that day.

Although Mahadev Bhai was exuding a sense of composure, a discerning eye would notice the faint lines of concern etched on his forehead. Mansukh appeared just as concerned about the issue; he fully grasped his father's emotions.

Mahadev Bhai's wife, Maniben, patiently waited inside, but their young children happily ran to the door when he reached home. The younger brothers and sisters surrounded Mansukh, hoping their father might have bought them something special to eat, like *mithai ki goliyan* or fresh sweets. During those times, children would be content in this manner, but it was still a challenge for parents to arrange it quite often. Mahadev Bhai's children mostly used to get such disappointments, and that day was no different.

In the past, women stayed in *purdah,* but they still asked their husbands about their day's happenings in a low and timid voice. When Maniben asked about his daily earnings, he shook his head dejectedly. Mahadev Bhai placed some coins from the long pocket of his *kurta* on the table in front of the pictures of gods and goddesses. Those were the earnings for the day.

Mahadev Bhai and Maniben lived in their small mud house. British colonial rule's exploitative nature and practices made it difficult for rural people to make ends meet. Across the country, people in rural areas faced the same hardships, not to mention job opportunities. Although Mahadev Bhai delivered goods to customers with a smile every day, deep inside, he was worried about the future. Mahadev Bhai's elders had always advised him, *'You should cut your coat according to your clothes,'* but now he was facing a new dilemma as his clothes were getting shorter and shorter. *His earnings were like a drop in the ocean, while his family's needs were like a mountain.*

Mahadev Bhai was very sad that he could not educate his eldest child, Mansukh, beyond Class Five because he could not afford to send him away from the village for education. After that, Mansukh started helping in the shop. The other children in the family too grew old enough to attend school. In addition to their upbringing, worry about their education expenses did not allow Mahadev Bhai to live peacefully.

Mahadev Bhai explored various options to tackle the increasingly severe economic crisis in the family, but no viable solution existed. Narali was a poverty-stricken village where the purchasing power of the locals was so limited that they could only afford to buy food enough to fill their stomachs. Even the simple task of grocery shopping became a challenge for them. It's heart-wrenching to think about, isn't it? In such a scary scenario, there was no point in expanding the small grocery shop, either with or without arranging money from blood-sucking money lenders.

The second option that kept coming to Mahadev Bhai's mind repeatedly was to leave the village, go to a more prominent place, and earn a living. But it was not practical at all. The British atrocities were on the rise as India's freedom struggle was approaching its pinnacle. The decade spanning from 1930 to 1940 was a significant period in India's freedom movement, marked by several historic events.

These included the executions of martyrs Bhagat Singh, Sukhdev, and Rajguru, the Civil Disobedience Movement, the Dandi March, the ban on the Congress Committee, and the imprisonment of Jawaharlal Nehru and Mahatma Gandhi. Additionally, the decade saw the signing of the Gandhi-Irwin Pact. Ruthless policies of British rule sent the whole country into turmoil. Mahadev Bhai was caught in a vicious cycle of poverty, as he could neither go outside in search of better opportunities nor expand his small shop. The circumstances were so harsh that it looked as if all the odds were stacked against him. As Mahadev Bhai struggled hard, the years passed, but nothing changed.

Greek Stoic philosopher Epictetus once said, "*No great thing is created suddenly, any more than a bunch of grapes or a fig. If you tell me that you desire a fig, I answer that there must be time. Let it first blossom, then bear fruit, then ripen.*" Mahadev Bhai never imagined that his ten-year-old son, Mansukh, would one day create history. A large number of books have been written on the adverse effects of poverty on children, including their future aspirations, mental health, and ability to form strong friendships, but what made Mansukh stand out from the rest was his extraordinary character. He had the ability to shine in any situation. Adversity has the power to break us down or make us stronger. In Mansukh Bhai's case, it made him mentally tough as steel. He didn't allow the hardships to weaken him. Instead, he used them as a catalyst to become even stronger. Mansukh Bhai's unrelenting desire to transform his circumstances was deeply ingrained in him during his formative years. The rest is history.

2

Diamond in the Rough

"A gem cannot be polished without friction,
nor a man perfected without trials."

– Lucius Annaeus Seneca, Stoic Philosopher of Ancient Rome

A prodigy can achieve extraordinary success, regardless of a humble background, surroundings, or a life full of hardships. Some children are born with unique qualities that make them as valuable as diamonds. However, they need to be polished to shine. Mansukh Bhai's sharp intellect manifested itself even in childhood, as he could discern the pain etched on his father's face. This innate ability to read emotions and body language was a valuable trait that he carried with him throughout his life, making him an astute and perceptive individual.

Have you ever heard of an eighteen-year-old with eight years of work experience? It may sound strange, but it was true in the case of Mansukh Bhai.

Due to financial constraints, he was unable to study much during his childhood. As a result, when he was only ten years old, he began assisting his father in his grocery shop. Despite the difficulties he faced in life, he was moulded into an incredible person by his parents' values and the struggles he encountered. He started craving to break the shackles of poverty at an age when most children were still playing with dolls and toys. There is no doubt that he was a hidden diamond.

A hundred years ago...

Surendranagar district is a region located in the Indian state of Gujarat. It is known for its thriving cotton industry, numerous pharmaceutical companies, and other industrial sectors that have contributed significantly to the region's economic growth. However, hundred years ago, in 1925, the district was the headquarters of the British Political Agent for Wadhawan. The area's population was relatively small then, and the people's welfare and the region's development were never a priority for the British. In the early 1900s, life in rural areas was tough due to the scarcity of basic amenities like electricity, roads, healthcare, and education. This was particularly true for the underprivileged village of Narali, where Mansukh Bhai was born in 1925. (In the past, many children were born at home and their parents did not always keep track of their birth dates.)

The cries of the couple's first child echoed through the courtyard, a joyous sound that was celebrated by the entire village with folk songs. For Mahadev Bhai and Maniben, the birth of their son brought an endless wellspring of happiness; the couple named their child Mansukh, a fitting tribute to the love and blessings surrounding his birth. The couple struggled to survive on meagre earnings, and their daily existence was a relentless battle. Though the arrival of their child brought a glimmer of hope, their hardships persisted. Yet, through it all, the child's playful laughter infused their dreary surroundings with vitality. And so, years passed, the couple's struggles undiminished.

When Mansukh was five years old, his father, Mahadev Bhai, faced a dilemma about his education. Only government schools existed then; private schools did not exist even in the imagination. Therefore, Mahadev Bhai admitted his son to a primary school near their village. However, the school building was dilapidated. The building only had a thatched roof and brick floor but needed a proper seating arrangement. The children had to bring their own sackcloth, and those who could not get it had to sit on the littered floor. The school remained closed on rainy days because the building was often wet or filled with water. Despite these conditions, the children managed to sit and learn. In those days, the teachers were called *Massab,* they wore long coats and *dhotis* and despite limited resources, teachers worked tirelessly to provide a strong educational foundation for children.

The wisdom of the ages has given us a powerful message through a Hindi saying, *"Honhar birwan ke hot chikne paat",* which highlights that the talent of a gifted child becomes apparent from an early age. This is perfectly illustrated by the story of young Mansukh, whose exceptional aptitude for counting and tables astounded his teachers. Everything was going well for Mansukh. He had a remarkable ability to memorize study lessons quickly, making him a favourite among his teachers and a leader among his classmates. His teachers repeatedly advised his father, Mahadev Bhai, to send him for further studies. However, fate had other plans, and Mansukh's studies stopped after Class Five. Mahadev Bhai recognized the value of education and wished for his son, Mansukh, to attend a city school. However, he was facing financial difficulties and could not afford it. In the absence of a large school in the village, Mansukh would have had to travel approximately 30 kilometres to continue his education, which was a cause of concern for Mahadev Bhai due to the lack of transportation and safety issues. After much deliberation with his wife, Mahadev Bhai made the difficult decision to discontinue Mansukh's education. It was a heavy-hearted decision, but given the challenging circumstances, it was the only practical option.

No one can stop the unstoppable force of a true genius. Despite having his education cut short, Mansukh Bhai's unwavering passion for learning never faded. At the age of ten, he started helping his father in the shop, where he acquired fundamental business skills and gained a wealth of valuable knowledge and experience.

Foundation of values

The foundation of one's values is laid during childhood. A mother with a loving heart takes excellent care to ensure the all-round development of her children, regardless of her circumstances. Maniben deeply understood religious literature and instilled values in her son by narrating stories from *Ramayana* and *Mahabharata.* Mansukh Bhai would always listen to such stories attentively, and gradually, he was deeply influenced by the character of Lord Ram. He learned that fulfilling the duty of a son was not enough; he wanted to go beyond and serve his parents by fulfilling all their wishes. After hearing the story of Shravan Kumar, he was motivated to work hard to achieve this goal. Thus, the seeds of hard work, courage, mutual love, and values were sown in him at such a tender age.

As we know, Mansukh Bhai had a tough childhood; his parents were always working hard. His mother spent her mornings in the kitchen while his father ran the shop. Mansukh Bhai found it challenging to think for himself despite being an exceptional child. He often forgot about his needs and desires, seeing how much his parents were struggling. He had to adapt to challenging circumstances, and there was no time to enjoy a carefree childhood with fairy tales or toys.

Learning the value of hard work

Although Mansukh Bhai's formal education was limited to primary schooling, his proficiency in household and shop work quickly became remarkable. His father made it a point to inculcate in him the belief that the ultimate triumph of a business is in catering to the needs of its customers. Mansukh Bhai learned in childhood that *a customer-centric approach is essential to advance in business.*

As someone rightly said, "Be curious. Keep your eyes and mind open to things you may not even know exist. That's an essential part of learning and growing. The more you're willing to ask, the more you'll get out of it." Since joining his father's shop, Mansukh Bhai had an exceptional curiosity and an undiminished passion for learning the intricacies of business. Five years went by. Mansukh was fifteen now. Once, he accompanied his father to the weekly market. He was eager to learn how to purchase goods, understand their origins, and how they were brought to the market. Unfortunately, his father was too busy bargaining and purchasing to teach him much. However, Mansukh Bhai learned a valuable lesson from the experience. He realized that his father's wise and hardworking approach to buying goods led to purchases at reasonable rates. This experience taught Mansukh Bhai the importance of working hard and being diligent to succeed in all aspects of life.

"A horse and the fifteen-mile walk"

Mahadev Bhai had to travel 15 miles from his home to buy groceries for his shop. He had to make this journey in all seasons, whether winter, summer, or rainy. Unfortunately, no motor or bus service was available. So, initially, he had to walk long distances. This was a challenging task, especially during the rainy season, when he feared he might slip and fall into the water. To avoid such dangers, Mahadev Bhai later decided to keep a horse to make these trips easier and safer. However, he could only use the horse for one side of the journey. Mahadev Bhai was a kind-hearted man who took great care of animals. He never overloaded his horse or rode on its back when goods were transported. Instead, he always walked alongside the horse on their way back from the market. Although this meant a long and tiring journey, Mahadev Bhai always remained calm and patient. When Mansukh Bhai accompanied his father to the market, he would ride the horse there, but on the way back, they both walked. Despite the long walks causing his father great pain, Mansukh Bhai noticed that he never complained. *His father's resilience and determination to keep going without stopping inspired Mansukh Bhai to develop a strong work ethic in his teenage years.*

Skilled in counting and honest in accounting

Once, Mansukh Bhai went to the shop in the morning and returned in the evening after updating the book of accounts. A little later, his father came home and scattered currency coins of small denominations among the cots in the courtyard. While Mansukh immediately started counting them, his mother kept looking at them. The younger brother watched on in amazement from a distance. Mahadev Bhai was pleased to see his son counting the coins fast and accurately. With a sense of pride, he said, "Mansukh, make sure to count the coins accurately before filling them into bags. We need to bring goods from the market next week." Mansukh Bhai was not only perfect in counting but also honest in accounting. As told by his father, Mansukh Bhai never added extra money to the accounts of those customers who took goods on credit.

Additionally, no discrepancies were ever discovered in any other accounts. Mahadev Bhai strongly believed in treating all customers equally, whether big or small. *These ethical business values were instilled in Mansukh Bhai from the very start.*

Yearning to do something big

Mansukh Bhai grew up helping his family run their shop, but things only got more demanding as time went on. Despite his exceptional qualities, he never felt the need to prove his worth to anyone. Instead, he concentrated on enhancing his family's monetary condition and bringing joy to his parents. Seeing his father's struggles often left Mansukh Bhai feeling a bit frustrated and even tearful at times, but he never gave up. Instead, he found solace in new ideas and ways to move forward.

Whenever he heard something from his father, his ongoing process of ideological brainstorming would come to a stop. Sometimes, he would feel angry inside, clench his fists, or tighten his jaw. However, he could not find any way to improve the problematic situation, which left him exhausted when he returned home. Even during great uncertainty, he remained calm and helped his mother with household chores to keep her in good spirits. He would fill water, run the flour grinding mill, and even work with his mother to plaster and paint the house. He believed that all work, no matter how big or small, deserved equal dedication until completion. Mansukh Bhai later used to advise, *"Make work an addiction, and money will come naturally."*

Mansukh Bhai grew up to become a confident young man despite all his hardships as he turned eighteen. His struggles forced him to mature faster than most, increasing his determination to overcome his difficulties. His unwavering resolve to break free from the chains of adversity had reached its peak, and he was ready to tackle any obstacle that stood in his way. With a heart full of courage and a mind full of determination, Mansukh Bhai was determined to rise above his circumstances and carve out a better future. Despite facing several challenges, he always strongly desired to change his parents' lives positively. He initially had two ideas – the first was to expand his father's shop, and the second was to start farming. However, he faced a significant hurdle with the farming idea due to the area's high cost of seeds and materials and a severe water shortage. As a result, he decided to abandon the farming idea. Although he had doubts about expanding the shop due to the limited number of buyers in the village, he knew he had to do something to improve his family's financial situation. He needed capital to expand the shop, which, unfortunately, was unavailable. He was aware of his father's financial condition and knew he had to find a way to make his dream a reality.

He knew he had to act fast!

Have you ever found yourself feeling unsure of which direction to take in life? When he was eighteen years old, Mansukh Bhai found himself in this very situation. It was then that he remembered his maternal uncle who lived in Kanpur. Although his uncle hadn't achieved the expected success in the textile business, his family's financial condition had improved. This inspired Mansukh Bhai to consider leaving home to do something, but he was torn between following his uncle's footsteps and running their family grocery shop and helping his parents. For many days, he struggled to make a decision.

Mandy Hale, a renowned author, once said, "It can be painful to undergo change, but it's far more painful to be stuck in a place where you don't belong." Mansukh Bhai was a visionary who realized in 1943 that none of the available options for improving the living conditions in his village were viable. After weeks of turmoil in his mind, he was inspired by God to leave the village and seek a better life elsewhere. Mansukh Bhai realized he needed to leave his village to secure a better future for his family. He faced various challenges, even as a teenager, and never had the chance to be comfortable. The only thing that truly worried him was the thought of living without his parents' love, affection, and care.

Sometimes, we must make difficult choices and sacrifices for the greater good. This was the case for Mansukh Bhai, who had to take on the responsibility of his parents and seven younger siblings at a very young age. While his siblings played and laughed in their home courtyard, Mansukh Bhai knew their family's happiness was in danger. Their financial situation was dire. Mansukh Bhai couldn't just sit by and watch his family suffer. He knew he had to act fast.

A diamond shines with unparalleled brilliance after undergoing a rigorous process of refinement. Similarly, Mansukh Bhai's upbringing and unimaginable struggles instilled invaluable values that shaped him into a remarkable individual. It was hard to believe that this exceptional person would go on to outshine his peers in the business world and become a true legend.

CAWNPORE

3

First Step towards a Long Journey

"Decision is the spark that ignites action. Until a decision is made, nothing happens.... Decision is the courageous facing of issues, knowing that if they are not faced, problems will remain forever unanswered."

– Wilfred Peterson, American Author

Mansukh Bhai had decided to leave his village to look for better opportunities. However, he knew it would be difficult to convince his parents to let him go. It was 1943, a year after the Quit India Movement had started. The British were increasing their oppression to suppress the movement and maintain their power over India. As the Second World War raged on, the eastern province of Bengal was hit by a severe famine that claimed the lives of three million people. In these uncertain times, many parents hesitated to let their children leave for other cities in search of a better future.

The distance between Surendranagar and Kanpur is still around 1300-1400 km by train. In those days, embarking on a journey of such magnitude and dreaming of a better future was like starting anew in a strange land. But despite all the logistical and financial challenges, Mansukh Bhai was determined to visit Kanpur, known as the Manchester of the North. He knew he had to explore opportunities beyond the status quo. Despite his family's financial struggles, he refused to let them hinder his dreams. With a deep sense of courage and faith in God, he mustered the courage to tell his father about his plan. He knew it would not be easy, but he believed that with his father's support, he could make it happen.

Mansukh Bhai told his father, "*Pitaji,* I can't handle the financial crisis at our grocery store anymore. I want to go to the city and work hard to earn more money. This will help us improve our financial condition," he said with a sigh.

Mahadev Bhai was fully engaged in his son's words, his eyes widening with every passing moment. Suddenly, he let out an exclamation of surprise, clearly taken aback by what he had just heard. He exclaimed, "Hey!"

"What did you say? Journey to which city?" asked Mahadev Bhai.

Mansukh Bhai replied, "Kanpur city!"

"Why Kanpur? What are you hoping to discover there? Are you familiar with the location and do you have sufficient funds to get there?" Mahadev Bhai asked with a curiosity.

Mahadev Bhai asked a series of sharp questions, not stopping until he was trembling with anger. He questioned his son about why he couldn't see how people were protesting against the British outside, where he would go, and with whom he would stay. When Mansukh Bhai mentioned staying with relatives in Kanpur, Mahadev Bhai asked if they would keep him. After bombarding his son with questions, he cried deep inside his heart over his situation. He felt that his son would not have thought of such a plan if their financial conditions had been better. To hide his weakness, he went outside the room of their kutcha house.

Mahadev Bhai began to console himself by saying, "It doesn't matter for now. I'm getting late for the shop. I'll think about it again if I get the time." Once he reached this point, he walked towards the shop without saying anything to anyone.

Mansukh Bhai was finding it difficult to approach his father again as he assumed that his father would refuse to listen even if he attempted to initiate a conversation. Mahadev Bhai was known to be a man of few words and often responded only with a 'yes' or 'no'. Mansukh Bhai felt burdened by the weight of his thoughts until his mother called him for food.

Mansukh Bhai's determination was truly admirable. Despite the difficulty of carrying food from the kitchen to the shop for his father after such a conversation, he braved the challenge. With his father's words still ringing in his ears, he gathered the courage to face him. Upon reaching the shop, his father's reaction was stoic, but both father and son were soon engrossed in attending to a customer who had arrived. Mahadev Bhai watched his son work with agility and was impressed by his skills.

Mahadev Bhai was thinking about his son's words and he realized that people were not buying more because of their financial difficulties. The family was struggling to make ends meet as their children were growing up. After taking all of these factors into consideration, Mahadev Bhai surrendered the matter to God's hands. Once the customer had left, he called Mansukh Bhai to speak with him again.

Mahadev Bhai said to Mansukh, "Listen carefully. If your mother does not object, you can go to Kanpur. I will take care of the shop while you're away. However, make sure you plan your trip well and do not leave in a hurry. Let's go to the weekly market together and buy the necessary goods for the shop. While we're there, we can ask Lala from the other shop to help us find the train that goes to Kanpur."

Mansukh Bhai was all ears as he attentively listened to his father agreeing with his dreams. Though he was going to leave his home for the first time and travel to Kanpur, he wasn't feeling nervous. In fact, he was feeling thrilled to have received permission to go. As he imagined the future, Mansukh Bhai's dreams began to take flight.

Emotional moments with mother...

That night, Mansukh Bhai arrived at his mother Maniben's bedside. Every night before sleeping, he used to comfort his mother by pressing her forehead and feet, but that evening, things were different.

Maniben said, "Let it be. You must be tired too. Your father has already gone to bed, and you should go as well. You have to go to the shop again tomorrow."

Mansukh Bhai couldn't stop listening to his mother's sweet words, full of innocence, as she was unaware of his big decision. Finally, he gathered the courage to share his decision with her by saying, "Mother, I want to go to the city of Kanpur."

Maniben was about to sleep but attentively absorbed Mansukh Bhai's words.

"Maa, please don't refuse. You know how much this means to me," pleaded Mansukh Bhai, pouring his heart out.

As soon as Mansukh Bhai stopped talking, Maniben suddenly got up and sat down. She continued to look at Mansukh's face while caressing it. Even though they didn't say a word, tears streamed down their cheeks like the Ganga and Jamuna rivers. Mansukh Bhai was Maniben's first child, and seeing his mother cry, he also started to cry. They gazed at each other for a while, each crying silently. Even tears have their own story.

Maniben pretended to be angry the following day as she spoke to her son. "I've already told you that you can't go anywhere," she said. "Kanpur isn't nearby, and have you considered how I'll manage without you? If you have any problems, please tell me. If you can't tell me, tell your father. But do not go to Kanpur. I mean it."

Maniben managed to compose herself after some time and comforted her son. She kept stroking his hair and hugging him tightly while patting his back. Mansukh Bhai also embraced her dearly. He fondly reminisced all the moments spent with his mother. She used to wake him up in the morning and serve him breakfast. Whenever he got injured, she would quickly bring *haldi* and *chuna* to heal him, and how often, her dish of pulses cooking on the gas stove got burned while she was taking care of him. She used to tell him fairy tales and religious stories until he fell asleep, and she sometimes stayed awake to save him from mosquito bites.

The family's financial crisis was the reason for Mansukh Bhai's tough decision to go to Kanpur. Maniben thought such a situation would not have arisen if everything had been fine at home. She felt furious at herself, wondering when the bad days would end. After thinking about it repeatedly, she felt sad that the same problem had persisted for her eldest son from childhood to adulthood. Even during major festivals, sweets did not make their way into the house. His childhood had been a struggle, and now his youth was plagued by the same issues. She wondered what fate held for her son in Kanpur and whether he would be able to eat and live properly there.

The morning after, the sky was overcast, and Mahadev Bhai woke up early, perhaps concerned about Mansukh's journey to Kanpur. Maniben had already risen but was occupied with household tasks. Then Mahadev Bhai went to his shop. As it was a gloomy day, he returned home from his shop a little earlier than usual. After seeing his wife's face, he wanted to say something, but they both remained quiet. Maniben urged him to wash his hands, but he stood still, holding onto the veranda pole. Maniben noticed his behaviour and went inside to get him some water. In the past, women were often expected to remain silent and only cater to their husband's emotional needs.

Mahadev Bhai was pondering over the expenses he would incur to send his son to Kanpur. He wanted to plan his finances accordingly and was curious about the fare. Meanwhile, Mansukh Bhai's mother felt sad after hearing about her son's scheduled departure to Kanpur. She was busy with household chores all day and hardly paid attention to anything else. After sitting with her husband for a while, she realized that he was in a troubled state of mind. To console herself, she began discussing the matter with him, and upon seeing him staring blankly, she forgot her own pain.

Maniben said, "You work very hard, but despite your efforts, our financial condition is not improving. Your son is growing up and has his own desires, but we must find a way to manage. We will do our best, and hope that with God's help, things will get better."

Mahadev Bhai said, "As you can see, we are somehow managing to cover all our expenses. I also wanted my son to receive a good education and earn a decent living, but I'm not sure what to do. He expressed his desire to go to Kanpur."

"And listen. Now, I want him to go to Kanpur. Kanpur is a good, big, and affordable city. Many of our relatives live there and do business. Perhaps Mansukh could also find work. There's nothing left here. I've spent my life counting from one to sixteen *annas,* but the situation remains the same. The expenses continue to increase, but the income remains the same. I don't even know what to do anymore."

"I've already decided. If you don't have any objections, then we'll happily send him off to Kanpur. Perhaps Kanpur could change his luck." Having said that, Mahadev Bhai went silent. He looked down at the ground and began to think about something."

In the meantime, Mansukh Bhai also arrived, and it took him some time to understand the situation. To lighten the mood, he told his mother that he was going to Kanpur to visit Mamaji and would stay there for a few days. Mansukh Bhai assured his mother, saying, "Maa, there's no need to worry. Although no one in our family has ever travelled to Kanpur, I promise you I'll be fine. Please bless me, and I assure you that I will return soon. I understand your concerns about Pitaji managing the shop alone. How long do you think he can handle it? Don't worry, I'll take care of everything and come back as soon as possible."

Maniben found solace in the thought that her son would return home after staying at his Mama's place, as whatever he said would happen. She believed that this would help relieve his mind a little. There was a telepathic communication between Mansukh Bhai's parents, as whatever the father was thinking, the mother was thinking in almost the same direction.

After receiving approval from his parents, Mansukh Bhai sought their blessings the following day. He prepared to pursue his goal without considering the potential challenges, knowing that *success cannot be attained without persevering through struggles.*

Unlike today, railway stations did not provide passengers with food or water in the past. Additionally, the train's engine needed to be changed at several locations, which Mansukh Bhai was unaware of. Even with all the relevant information available at the click of a mouse today, most young people would not travel to a distant city they hardly know. However, Mansukh Bhai was different. Rather than giving up, his challenges and difficulties inspired him to take the first big step towards a long journey. Somewhere deep inside his heart, he had the spark that he would be able to turn the tide in his favour. The most valuable assets that Mansukh Bhai carried with him from his village were the human values and business principles he had learned during childhood. *It is said that those who make an effort always succeed.*

4

Not Just a Journey, But a Turning Point

Decision making is power. Most people don't have the guts to make a 'tough decision' because they want to make the 'right decision' and so they make 'no decision'. Remember, life is short, so do things that matter the most and have the courage to make 'tough decisions' and to chase your dreams.

— *Yama Mubtakeraker, Philanthropist*

Mansukh Bhai was setting out on a new path in his life, aware that the journey ahead would be extremely arduous. He knew the difficulties and challenges that awaited him, but he was determined to succeed. Mansukh Bhai believed that he was being tested before he could attain success. However, he was content that he could bring happiness to his parents by doing good work in the city. He refused to resign himself to fate and instead chose to take charge of his life.

Before leaving home for the railway station, Mother applied a tilak on Mansukh Bhai's forehead and kissed him with deep love. Mansukh Bhai and his father left for Viramgam Junction, the only station in Surendranagar. Mahadev Bhai brought the horse. He used to ride this horse to buy goods from the market, but today was different. He asked Mansukh to sit on the horse, but Mansukh requested his father to sit on the horse. Neither Mahadev Bhai nor Mansukh Bhai sat on the horse. Father held the horse rope in his hand, and Mansukh Bhai left the house with the bag for the journey, a journey that had already begun, although its end was unknown.

There were few people at Viramgam station. Mahadev Bhai offered to take his son's small bag, but Mansukh Bhai refused, saying, "There's no weight to it. I'll carry it myself. Don't worry Pitaji."

A stream of tears...

Mahadev Bhai stopped his son on the platform and went to buy a ticket for him. He spoke to Mansukh Bhai for a while, explaining as much as he could about the difficulties his son might face on the way. As Mahadev Bhai waited for the train to arrive, he braced himself for what would come. When it finally pulled in, he knew he had to remain strong. But sometimes, things are not in our control, and deep emotions overpower us. He gave his son the ticket and some money before bidding him farewell.

Mansukh Bhai got into a relatively quiet compartment. When the train's whistle blew, Mahadev Bhai started crying, even though he didn't want to. Tears streamed down his face, and Mansukh Bhai also began to cry. The separation between father and son was heart-wrenching. As the train started to move, Mahadev Bhai walked alongside it for a few steps. Then, as the train picked up speed, he slowly stopped walking but kept looking at it until it had crossed the entire platform and disappeared from sight. Although the father may appear harsh on the outside, his eyes are the window to the soul. Behind those eyes lies an untold story containing billions of tears. The eyes reveal everything. It was difficult for Mahadev Bhai to control his emotions.

The train was moving at its usual speed towards Kanpur, and Mansukh Bhai was feeling tired and homesick. His thoughts were preoccupied with his parents. To take a break, he bought a one-anna tea. While sipping his tea, he noticed a group of people arguing over a seat. Mansukh Bhai observed the scene for a while but decided to intervene. He raised his voice and told the gentleman, "Brother, why are you quarrelling? I will get up, and you can sit. We all have to reach our destination by this train. We can't go home without taking the train. I will get off at Kanpur, and you will get off somewhere else. *Let's focus on the destination, not on the means of getting there.*" Mansukh Bhai's few words carried a profound message, and little did he know then that those words would become the guiding principle of his life.

After some time, Mansukh Bhai fell asleep while sitting. As the night wore on, he started having difficulty sleeping. However, Mansukh Bhai did not ask anyone to vacate his seat. Instead, he spread his towel on the train floor and slept. He could have asked someone to move, but it was not in Mansukh Bhai's values to trouble anyone. Therefore, he chose to sleep on the floor instead of reacting angrily to someone else resting on his seat.

The next day, a man with a limp boarded the train with a bag of peanuts. Some of the passengers seated around Mansukh Bhai started eating the peanuts. A woman seated nearby with her children scolded them when they asked for some, perhaps because she had no money to buy.

This situation reminded Mansukh Bhai of his childhood when his family sometimes struggled to afford enough food. Despite this, his mother always made sure he felt like he had enough to eat. As the children kept asking for peanuts, Mansukh Bhai's heart melted, and he decided to show kindness to them. He took out two paise from his pocket and bought some peanuts for the children. The kids were overjoyed and started to eat them with great enthusiasm.

A peanut-seller, and a business mantra!

Mansukh Bhai had an innate inclination towards continuous learning, which ran in his DNA. He began learning from his family and the shop and continued this habit when he travelled for the first time. He even learned some valuable business mantras from the peanut seller. When the peanut seller grew tired and stood near the door, Mansukh Bhai joined him and began a conversation. Using his impressive communication skills, he gleaned complete information from the peanut seller about where he sourced his peanuts, how much he brought, how far he travelled in a day, and how he earned a profit. Mansukh Bhai listened attentively and memorized his words like a business mantra. He was a great learner and always took something away from every person he spoke with. In his later years, Mansukh Bhai often said, *"Talking to people and always learning something new is very important for success."*

A compassionate heart

Mansukh Bhai noticed a ragged beggar on the train and felt great sympathy for him. He was taught to always help others, even if it meant sacrificing his own needs. Although he had only a few rupees, he still wanted to help the beggar. However, he hesitated because he didn't have enough money to give him. Suddenly, a voice inside him advised against giving the beggar money. But Mansukh Bhai was still compassionate and wanted to help the beggar in any way he could. He offered the beggar some food instead, and the beggar accepted gratefully. After taking a *thepla,* the beggar left with many blessings. Mansukh

Bhai then thought about his future and the possibility of facing a similar situation. However, he quickly reminded himself that everything would be fine and that he should not think negatively. He remembered his father's advice to *always keep moving forward.*

Mansukh Bhai's train finally arrived in Kanpur after a long journey. Although late, he was relieved to have reached his destination. However, he faced a new challenge – figuring out where to go next. He needed to find his maternal uncle, but he had no contact information besides his uncle's address written on a slip of paper. After some contemplation, he summoned a porter for assistance. He left the station with their guidance and approached the locals for additional help. After receiving directions, he realized his uncle's house was far away. Although he could have taken a horse-drawn carriage, he opted to walk instead. By doing so, he hoped to learn more about the city and its surroundings. Mansukh Bhai's natural foresight served him well in all aspects of life, including his work, thoughts, and opinions.

An award-winning innovator once said that *success and happiness lie beyond fear and that bravery and enduring faith take you there.* As he strode through the unfamiliar city, he exuded confidence. Eventually, he arrived at his uncle's house, who had just returned from work in the evening. Upon seeing him, his uncle's eyes lit up with joy, and he danced around in excitement before tightly embracing him in a warm hug.

Despite the obstacles ahead, Mansukh Bhai was undaunted and ready to confront them head-on. His unrelenting resolve and unwavering fortitude were his greatest strengths, and with these by his side, he was confident that he would emerge victorious.

With just fourteen rupees in his pocket!

Mansukh Bhai's story of success is awe-inspiring and truly unmatched. Though he had left his village with only fourteen rupees in his pocket, he transformed his humble beginning into a business empire. The significance of his initial investment cannot be understated. In today's context, let's calculate this amount to the equivalent value of gold. Historical data indicates that in 1943, 24-carat gold cost Rs 51 for 10 grams. He could have purchased about three grams of gold with fourteen rupees. Today (21 April 2024), three grams of 24 carat gold would be worth around Rs. 22,000/-, so his initial investment would have been worth only Rs. 22,000/- today. Yet, he overcame this obstacle and touched the stars through hard work and determination. Mansukh Bhai's journey is a true testament to the power of perseverance.

The art of learning was in his DNA...

Mansukh Bhai's capacity to learn was extraordinary.

Learning was not just a habit for him; it was innate in his DNA. His father's work at the shop was a constant source of inspiration for him. He watched as his father and other people diligently brought goods from miles away, often on horseback or foot. Despite the long hours and hard work, his father never complained or let the feeling of tiredness get to him. Instead, he only believed in karma and starting afresh every day. This left an indelible impression on Mansukh Bhai, who learned the values of honesty and self-confidence from his father. Even in the face of difficulties, he never saw his father dissatisfied. Through these experiences, Mansukh Bhai developed his unique approach to learning, a method that he applied to his life with great success.

AVADI
AVADI

5

Building a Future, Brick-by-Brick

"Strength and growth come only through continuous effort and struggle."

—Napoleon Hill, American Self-Help Author

Since his early days, Mansukh Bhai faced numerous obstacles, but he never lost his determination to build a better future, one step at a time. Moving to a new and bustling city can be overwhelming, especially for young people who feel vulnerable and unsure of themselves. Yet, Mansukh Bhai refused to let his doubts hold him back. He had faith in his ability, and he was willing to work hard to achieve his goals. With a positive attitude and unwavering determination, Mansukh Bhai proved that anything is possible if you believe in yourself.

The following day in Kanpur, it was discovered that there was no hand pump in Mansukh Bhai's maternal uncle's house. This meant fetching water for daily activities and bathing was challenging, as it had to be sourced from a distant location. Mansukh Bhai managed to bring water for himself and his uncle despite this obstacle. This showcased his resourcefulness and highlighted his loving and caring nature towards his family. After a refreshing bath and breakfast, he left to explore job opportunities.

Mansukh Bhai was determined to only return to his maternal uncle's house when he found work. As he left, he couldn't help but worry about his parents. Mansukh Bhai tirelessly explored the city, starting from Ghantaghar and then Birhana Road, diligently inquiring about job opportunities at every establishment he encountered. Despite his unwavering determination, he faced negative responses at every turn. He went around the markets asking for jobs from shopkeepers, but things still needed to go his way. Mansukh Bhai had valuable experience running a shop with his father and was confident he could manage two meals a day if he secured a job in a shop. However, as the day progressed, his job search was disheartening, leaving him a bit frustrated by evening. Despite the setbacks, he didn't let his determination waver and continued looking for work. As we often say, *luck favours the brave.* On his way back, he approached a guard outside a company and inquired about any job openings.

Mansukh Bhai asked the guard, "Brother, what happens here?" The guard asked, "What do you want to know?" Mansukh Bhai replied, "Brother, can I get any work here?" Before the guard could answer, the head of the cleaning staff, who had arrived there, overheard their conversation and said, "If you have the ability to monitor cleanliness, then let me know."

First job, salary 80 paise per month!

Mansukh Bhai was overjoyed to receive a job offer, despite the meagre salary of 80 paise per month. He did not question the nature of the work and immediately accepted the offer. He shared the good news with his uncle, who initially doubted the suitability of the job but suggested he give it a try and look for other opportunities simultaneously. Mansukh Bhai's uncle advised him to leave the current job if he found a better one. Although his uncle could have offered him a job at his shop, he worked in a low position and did not consider it. Jobs were scarce, and salaries were paid only in *annas*. In September 1943, Mansukh Bhai began working as a cleanliness supervisor in the company, which was his first job since moving to Kanpur from Narali.

Counted bricks for one rupee and four annas per month!

While working as a cleanliness supervisor for several months, Mansukh Bhai kept an eye out for any job opportunities that might come his way. One day, he noticed a construction site nearby and observed the workers diligently performing their tasks, with many of them counting bricks. Out of curiosity, he approached one of the workers and asked, "Excuse me, may I ask what exactly is happening here?"

A worker said, "We are counting bricks." Then Mansukh Bhai asked, "Can I also get some work here?" The worker replied, "The contractor is sitting in front. Go and ask him." Mansukh Bhai approached the contractor and asked, "Can I also get some work?"

The contractor looked at Mansukh Bhai from head to toe and asked, "Can you count the bricks? Will you be able to keep a complete account?" To which Mansukh Bhai replied, "Yes, I will do whatever you say. How much will I get paid?" The contractor replied, "You will earn one rupee and four *annas* per month. However, you will receive your full salary only after working for a year."

Even one rupee and four annas were not a good salary; however, they were more than the cleaning company offered. The real problem was what he would eat if the salary was received after one year. How would he live? Mansukh Bhai pleaded with the contractor, "Look, brother, I have come all the way from Gujarat. I have nowhere to stay, and no money to eat. If you give me the money after a year, then how will I survive for a year?"

Coincidentally, the contractor was also Gujarati. Upon hearing Mansukh Bhai's concerns, the contractor offered him a seat and a glass of water and reassured that the payment from the *Hindustan Construction Company* would be made on time. He also offered to arrange for Mansukh Bhai's food and accommodation during his stay in Kanpur. The contractor suggested that Mansukh Bhai could have two full meals daily for a small amount of money, as food was relatively inexpensive in the area. Additionally, he provided Mansukh Bhai with some work and advised him to keep an eye on the workers, counting the bricks. Finally, he invited him to his room in the evening.

Mansukh Bhai started his second job at *Hindustan Construction Company* in January 1944. He felt proud of himself for accomplishing something he never thought possible, just a few days earlier. Mansukh Bhai carried his bag on his shoulder and began counting the daily shipment of bricks for a building the company was constructing. Later that evening, he went to the contractor's room, where the contractor inquired about his family and home and then offered him food.

Mansukh Bhai's dedication and honesty never went unnoticed. After collecting his dues as a cleaning supervisor at the company on Birhana Road, he formally started working for the contractor with complete commitment. On his first day, he impressed the contractor with his quick work speed, intellectual skills, and knowledge of tables he had learned from his school teacher, which he used for counting bricks. Mansukh Bhai's hard work and dedication paid off, and the contractor was pleased with his work when he submitted his accounts by evening. The contractor even served him *jalebi,* which filled Mansukh Bhai with immense joy. However, he couldn't help but remember his difficult village days when he couldn't afford to even look at sweet shops due to lack of money. *Despite the hardships, he held on to the moments spent with his parents and never forgot them, whether in happiness or sorrow.*

Crucial phase of life in Avadi, Karnataka

Mansukh Bhai's hard work and dedication earned him recognition from the officers of *Hindustan Construction Company.* They were so pleased with his work as a brick-counting man that they entrusted him with a crucial responsibility—managing a canteen in Avadi, Karnataka. The company had faced a food-related scandal in its canteen and needed someone honest and hardworking to restore its reputation. Mansukh Bhai, with his positive attitude and commitment to excellence, was the perfect fit for the role despite having no experience in canteen management.

The company provided him with a house to live in, and Mansukh Bhai decided to send the rent money to his father to improve their financial situation. He believed that hard work and dedication would eventually lead to success. This new phase of his life was crucial, as it taught him essential human resources and financial management skills.

In February 1945, Mansukh Bhai arrived in Avadi and immediately began working in the canteen. However, he was greeted by a poor system, dissatisfied cooks, and workers causing chaos over the food. Despite this challenge, he fearlessly began working in the canteen with a smile and took charge. To gain everyone's trust, he met with all the canteen staff to understand their problems. He then conducted a thorough inspection of the canteen after some time.

Quickly rose as a team leader

Mansukh Bhai had no experience managing teams, but he quickly developed himself as a team leader and motivated his employees. He assured them they were all perfect and working for a great company, but the only problem was the timing. He promised that if they worked together, they would be as happy as him in just a few days. This statement had a magical effect on the canteen employees, who started working the next day. Mansukh Bhai aimed to please the boss by cutting expenses without upsetting workers. He had a solution in mind.

The next day, Mansukh Bhai made a list of essential items for the canteen. He went to the market with one of the employees and managed to buy better quality goods at a lower cost than the company's budget had allowed for, as he was skilled in bargaining. He then tasted the canteen food himself before serving it to others. He incorporated some Gujarati and Kanpuri styles to enhance the taste of the food. Within four days, canteen sales increased, and the eating staff began to praise the food. Mansukh Bhai introduced many new dishes at the canteen, attracting more people and increasing the income. After reviewing the calculations for a month, the officers were pleased with Mansukh Bhai due to the reduced expenses and increased revenue. The canteen employees were also happy with the open working environment, fewer restrictions, and continuous guidance and praise from Mansukh

Bhai. Mansukh Bhai implemented the Gujarati formula, "*Gujarati naam, sayano kaam aur chokho daam,*" which means that if one has a good reputation, one can do good work and charge a fair price.

Mansukh Bhai achieved what most people take decades to accomplish when he was just twenty years old. He managed a canteen single-handedly and, in doing so, revolutionized the way of working in the Avadi area with his innovative approach. He would cycle to the vegetable market daily to bargain for better-quality produce and spices. He also sourced goods directly from farmers in the surrounding villages, learning about the economy, bargaining, and quality. *Mansukh Bhai's forward-thinking approach eliminated middlemen, which helped farmers get the total price for their produce. This indirectly worked towards the prosperity of the villages, making him a true servant of the country.* Despite being unaware of his impact, he lived by his father's words: "*If you work hard, you will surely get fruitful results.*" His outstanding work was highly appreciated in the canteen, and his monthly salary increased to ten rupees. However, destiny had something else in store for him.

Luck often inspires hardworking people to continuously explore new opportunities. However, despite making a profit, the *Hindustan Construction Company* decided to close the canteen of its Avadi branch. The company had less work, and the number of eaters was reduced due to the retrenchment of workers. Hence, even though the canteen was economically beneficial, its usefulness began to diminish. Mansukh Bhai was also asked to leave. Many employees were angry about the canteen closure, leaving several people distressed and out of work. Mansukh Bhai had planned to send money to his parents after coming to Avadi, but he was also saddened by the loss of his job. He had been saving well, but unfortunately, no one could predict the future. After a year of a good job, Mansukh Bhai felt a bit hopeless and thought, *It is true that the writings of destiny are difficult to comprehend, but it is important to always stay on the path of karma.*

A life-changing decision!

After the company canteen closed, Mansukh Bhai stayed in the Avadi company quarters for two days, searching for another job. Unfortunately, he faced two major hurdles: the language barrier and the inability to find a job that offered the same salary as his previous one. Although large companies in the area had canteens, there were no current job vacancies. As a result, Mansukh Bhai decided to return to Kanpur instead of going home, as he had little savings and didn't want to burden his family.

Mansukh Bhai, despite his financial constraints, was actively seeking employment. He went to Lucknow for three to four days to explore job opportunities, but unfortunately, he spent most of his savings and couldn't find a job. Nevertheless, Mansukh Bhai never lost hope and continued to strive towards a better future. His unwavering determination led him to take a bold step and start his own business in 1946, which proved to be a life-changing decision.

6

Scripting Success in Turbulent Times

"Turbulence that blows you to greatness is better than calmness that stalls you in mediocrity."

– Matshona Dhliwayo, Philosopher

In today's world, we are fortunate to have countless job opportunities and access to a wealth of information. However, the loss of a job can have a detrimental impact on one's self-esteem. Imagine how much more devastating job loss must have been in 1946 when India was still under colonial rule. Mansukh Bhai, who was just 21 then, had multiple problems; he was hundreds of miles away from the comfort of his home with no roof over his head and no one to support him. After 3 years of hard work, he was on the road again. Many people would have given up, but Mansukh Bhai had a remarkably different approach. Even in highly adverse circumstances, he bravely took the initiative to start his own business with his small savings and incentives.

Starting a journey enthusiastically is easy, but sustaining it through obstacles and challenges sets the successful ones apart from the rest. Mansukh Bhai was one such person who never gave up on his dreams. He chose to take the less travelled path and embarked on the entrepreneurship journey despite needing more capital and experience. Instead of settling for a job that could make ends meet, he worked tirelessly towards his goals and made his dreams a reality. He knew that hard work and commitment were the keys to success, and he never wavered in his belief. Even when faced with the challenges of starting a business in unknown cities like Lucknow and Kanpur, he persevered and worked hard to overcome them.

Renowned author and motivational speaker Brian Tracy believes continuous learning is the key to success in any field. Interestingly, Mansukh Bhai demonstrated this remarkable quality decades ago without formal training. He scripted his success story by embracing a growth mindset and a thirst for knowledge. Mansukh Bhai had always been a keen observer, even since childhood. During his trips to Lucknow-Kanpur, he noticed the hawkers were making a good profit. Being a quick learner and diligent implementer, he decided to try his hand at hawking himself. He also discovered that goods in Calcutta were much cheaper than in Kanpur and Lucknow, which could be sold at a higher price in these cities. With a careful count of his money, Mansukh Bhai made his way to Kolkata (known as Calcutta at that time).

In 1946, Mansukh Bhai embarked on a new phase of his life in Calcutta. After leaving his village three years ago, Mansukh Bhai faced numerous hardships while travelling to big cities. However, these travels equipped him with valuable business skills. When he arrived in Calcutta, he spent a little time exploring the city. He began by staying at a Gujarati hotel for just two rupees and consulted with the hotel staff to learn more about the city.

Mansukh Bhai's next stop was the cosmetics market, where he was shocked to discover that a cream that cost Rs. 3 in Lucknow was available only for Re 1 in Calcutta. He spent most of the day exploring different markets and gathering information on everything he could. Later that evening, he uncovered even more opportunities at the wholesale market. He learned that the same cream, which cost Re 1 in residential areas of Calcutta, was sold for 12 *annas* in the wholesale market.

With all the information he had gathered, Mansukh Bhai decided to solely focus on the cosmetics business. That evening, he returned to the hotel and made a well-laid plan for his hawking business.

Mansukh Bhai woke up early in the morning and took a bath with enthusiasm. He had biscuits for breakfast and walked to the wholesale market to save money. Despite walking for an hour, he didn't mind as he still preferred to save money. The market opened late, so Mansukh Bhai took a complete round to identify the shops that would be useful for his work. He believed in the mantra of *"Look, listen, understand, make a full blueprint in your mind and then work, after which the chances of success always increase."* This helped him to succeed in his work.

Mansukh Bhai walked into a beautifully decorated shop as soon as it opened. He paused to offer a prayer and missed his parents dearly. Being the day's first customer, he engaged the shopkeeper with his eloquent words, humorous nature, and sweet demeanour. Mansukh Bhai explained that he had little capital and no permanent shop or vehicle but had experience testing and selling goods. He expressed his willingness to work hard and assured the shopkeeper of his value as an asset to the business. He promised to continuously help the shopkeeper sell his goods if given a chance and requested his support in supplying goods at concessional rates. He was determined to make the most of the opportunity given to him.

When Mansukh Bhai requested, the shopkeeper instructed his servant to get the goods. Once inside the shop, Mansukh Bhai diligently examined the merchandise and jotted down the desired items on paper. The shopkeeper could tell from his demeanour that Mansukh Bhai was a confident and well-informed customer. When he was done, Mansukh handed over the list to the servant. He had made a careful selection of items that met his budget constraints. After the goods were packed, Mansukh Bhai politely asked the shopkeeper if he could offer a discount, saying, "Brother, you should also give some discount... I am your first customer today..."

Shopkeeper – "Okay, I can offer you a discount, but please consider buying from me only in the future."

Business research at just 21!

The shopkeeper was impressed by Mansukh Bhai's positive attitude and decided to take 25 rupees less than the bill amount. Mansukh Bhai had a natural talent for business, which he had inherited from his father. Since childhood, he had learned various business tricks by helping his father in the shop. He observed people hawking and knew which goods could be sold where, how much people could bargain for different goods, and how to make profits and save money. Instead of buying and selling all kinds of goods, he identified the goods sold and consumed in a particular area, observed people's spending patterns, and then brought similar goods to sell. This approach helped him sell his goods quickly while hawking. Mansukh Bhai had an exceptional talent for business research, even when he was only 21 years old. Well before starting his own business, he had already conducted thorough research, making him a visionary in his field. Mansukh Bhai had the unique ability to predict outcomes with remarkable accuracy, which set him apart from his peers in the business world. Later, he could easily forecast the next 5 to 10 years.

After collecting cosmetic items from the shop, Mansukh Bhai went to Calcutta's biscuits and toffees market. There, he bought goods worth Rs. 100. After packing the goods, he left for Lucknow directly from Calcutta. Upon reaching Lucknow, he stayed at the Rajbharti Hotel, where he had previously stayed after returning from Avadi. The hotel charged him a rent of Rs. 1.50 per day. Early morning, Mansukh Bhai bought two big bags from a market near the hotel. One bag contained cosmetics, while the other had biscuits, toffees, and other items. As he entered the nearby settlement to sell his goods, he remembered his parents and God. Women from many houses came out to see his products, and Mansukh Bhai showed them to everyone. He kept his profits low and began selling goods at affordable prices. By the afternoon, most of his goods were sold, and it seemed like some divine force was helping him. After having lunch at the hotel, Mansukh Bhai wanted to rest, but he decided to calculate the amount of goods he had sold and the amount of products yet to be sold. He learned this habit from his father, who used to calculate the shop's sales and income in the afternoon and evening.

Mansukh Bhai made some calculations on paper, adding and subtracting numbers. To his delight, he discovered that he had sold goods worth Rs. 100 in just 5 hours on the first day, making a significant profit. This income made him happy, and he continued working instead of taking a break. In the hot afternoon, Mansukh Bhai sold his goods while calling out to people. He didn't worry about hunger or thirst, and whenever he felt hungry, he ate a biscuit he had kept with him and asked for water from people before returning to work.

After finishing the day's sales, Mansukh Bhai returned to his hotel in the evening. He stored his merchandise, locked it up, and went out to eat. Later that night, he reviewed his sales for the day. He checked what was sold and what was left, noted it on paper, and counted the money. Upon analyzing his sales, he realized that he had sold goods worth Rs. 100 in the morning but only Rs. 50 in the afternoon. He wondered why this happened.

In business, analysis is crucial, as it provides inspiration to move forward. Mansukh Bhai thought for a while and discovered that many biscuits and toffees were sold in the morning because children were found everywhere. People, especially women, gave children a lot of biscuits and toffees, which meant that their sales were more due to children. In the afternoon, however, women bought more cosmetics because their children were in school then. Since the women had little money, they purchased cosmetic items only, resulting in lower sales than in the morning. *Nowadays, large firms work with business analysis agencies to gather information about what will be sold, how, and when. However, in 1946, Mansukh Bhai did this work,* using the lessons he learned as a child by observing his father in his shop. Even though he had not received any formal education or training, his sharp mind helped him succeed in business.

Mansukh Bhai's hard work and persistence paid off six days after starting his hawking business. Despite his challenges, he never let fatigue and despair take over his mind. He was thrilled to realize that he was making money, which made him forget all his sorrows. After purchasing goods worth Rs. 400 from Calcutta and selling everything within a week, he was left with a profit of Rs. 100. This success inspired him to return to Calcutta and build on his achievements. He remembered all the streets and people he had met on his previous trip, and *he realized that if his products were well-received or repeat orders were placed, it would lead to more sales.*

On his second visit to Calcutta, Mansukh Bhai bought more biscuits and cosmetic items based on his previous experience. He took very little quantity of toffees. Although the biscuits were sold out quickly, there was a lot of difficulty in selling the toffees. Mansukh Bhai sold goods that other shopkeepers used to sell in the markets of Lucknow for 1 rupee, i.e., 16 *annas,* for 12 *annas,* i.e., 4 *annas* less. Despite selling his goods at a lower price than the market rate, he could extract a margin from it. This was because Mansukh Bhai could bring goods from Calcutta at lower prices.

Furthermore, Mansukh Bhai maintained a lower margin than other shopkeepers. When cheaper goods of the same quality were available at the doorstep, who would not buy them? Mansukh Bhai always ensured that the goods he brought were of good quality. He learned from his father that if the goods were of good quality and the price was low, selling them was no problem. On the second trip, Mansukh Bhai brought goods worth Rs. 400, but he only had to spend Rs. 370 instead of Rs. 400 this time. The shopkeeper from whom he bought the goods gave him a more significant discount than last time.

Blisters on his hands... and a passion to succeed!

Mansukh Bhai was a highly motivated person with a strong desire to succeed. He was not bothered by physical discomfort and worked hard to achieve his goals. Soon, he began bringing hosiery goods as well from Calcutta to Lucknow. When he arrived at the old marketplaces for the first time with bags full of hosiery items, people automatically came to him to buy the goods. While moving around, he explored many new areas, which helped him discover new customers and identify new routes. However, carrying the heavy bags continuously gave him blisters on his hands. Despite the physical discomfort, he was pleased with the good sales. It took him about one and a half days more than it had, the previous time, to sell the goods, but he was happy to have sold everything.

He travelled back and forth between Calcutta and Lucknow for two months to sell his goods. During this time, he earned considerable money, leaving him with Rs. 400 and an equal amount of goods left to sell. One night, while considering different options to increase sales, he came up with a new idea: start a hawking business in Kanpur. He believed that this would bring him even more profit. During his next trip from Calcutta, he headed straight to Kanpur instead of Lucknow.

In Kanpur, he found even better buyers, mainly because many labourers lived in the area with their families. This meant that his cosmetics and biscuits sold out quickly. He even began bringing goods from Calcutta on credit, as he had built a reputation with the businessmen there. They eagerly awaited his arrival, knowing he would buy quality products to sell.

Another benefit in Kanpur was that, there, he spent less on accommodation and food than in Lucknow. As a result, his profits continued to increase, and he set his sights on making even more money. He travelled around Kanpur for two months, and every night, he counted his savings, separating the profit amount from the rest. His eyes sparkled every time he saw his profits grow.

Buying a used bicycle to avoid wasteful expenditure

After selling goods for six months, Mansukh Bhai's total income was around Rs. 1300. To transport his goods, he decided to buy a bicycle. Rather than purchasing a new one, he opted for an old bicycle for Rs. 80, as he believed in avoiding wasteful expenditure and had no place to keep a new bicycle. With the arrival of the bicycle, Mansukh Bhai's business started booming. Previously, he could only visit 4 to 5 localities daily to sell his goods, but now he started going to fairs and exploring new localities by bicycle. This significantly increased his income, and by the end of the year, he had earned approximately Rs. 2500. Mansukh Bhai's hard work paid off, and he became an experienced player in hawking goods. He learned new things and formed new relationships, which helped him in his business.

According to Mansukh Bhai, *a good salesman should possess certain qualities. He should always be truthful, willing to visit customers repeatedly, and able to deliver the goods on time as required. Additionally, he should be capable of doing business in cash and be polite and gentle when dealing with customers.*

By 1947, Mansukh Bhai had become a successful businessman who earned money on the go. With the country's freedom, the hopes and expectations of the people were high. Despite living a good life, Mansukh Bhai continued to work hard, and by the end of the year, he had saved up approximately Rs. 5000 from his hawking business. He stayed in constant touch with his father, Mahadev Bhai, who was pleased to hear about his son's progress. Mansukh Bhai regularly sent money home and kept himself updated on his family's condition through letters and telegrams. As time passed, he continued to work hard in Lucknow and Kanpur, and eventually, fate brought him new blessings in the form of a family life.

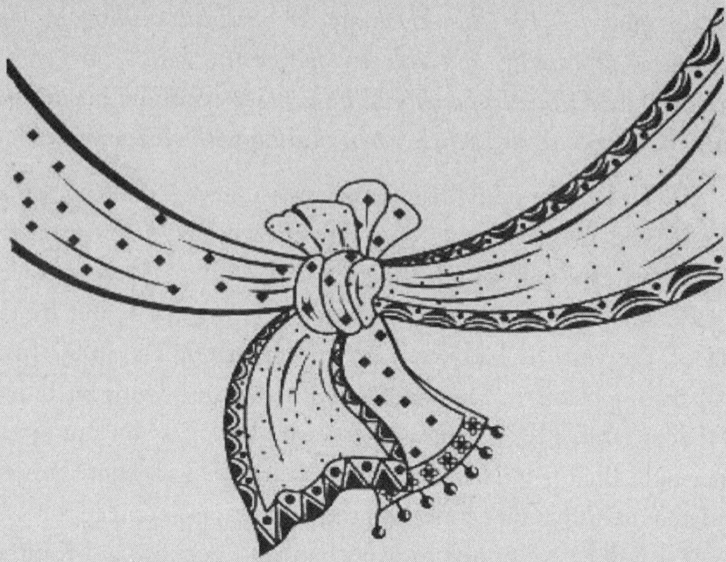

7

Better Together

"Happy is the man who finds a true friend, and far happier is he who finds that true friend in his wife."

– Franz Peter Schubert, Austrian Composer

Mahadev Bhai couldn't be prouder of his son's remarkable achievements in such a short period. Nonetheless, as a wise father, he knew the time had come for Mansukh Bhai to tie the knot. Mahadev Bhai believed that the *Grihastha Ashram* (married life) is a crucial stage where one learns to face every obstacle and crisis with one's own skills. This creates a sense of responsibility towards the family and helps maintain balance in life. The significance of *Grihastha Ashram* has been mentioned in our scriptures and, as a father, Mahadev Bhai, though not having read them, knew their essence. As proved 100 per cent right later, he was confident that his son would continue to excel in his personal and professional life with the support of an understanding partner.

Mahadev Bhai was concerned about finding a suitable marriage proposal for his son. He shared his thoughts with his wife one day. "Our son has matured and is taking on more responsibilities.

While you may have questions about his abilities, I have faith in him. Therefore, we should start looking for a suitable match for him."

Maniben said, "I never said that I have doubts about Mansukh's abilities. You talk strangely sometimes. There is always talk about the shop. When did you start worrying about me? Well, never mind. It's a good thing. I was also thinking the same thing, but I feared you might get angry if I discussed Mansukh's marriage." Maniben was thrilled to hear about the possibility of her son Mansukh's marriage. However, she wondered where they would find a suitable girl for him. Only then could the matter be resolved. Although the conversation was brief, there was tremendous excitement in the air.

The power of divine intervention has always been a subject of fascination for many. It is said that the Almighty has already charted the course of our lives, and when the time is right, things fall into place. A perfect example of this occurred at Mahadev Bhai's home. As they were considering the marriage of their son, Mansukh Bhai, a suitable proposal presented itself, almost as though it were meant to be. Mahadev Bhai said to himself, "The ways of the universe may be beyond our understanding, but it's moments like these that reinforce our faith in the power of destiny."

Incredible abilities that won him admiration

Mansukh Bhai possessed extraordinary abilities that left a lasting impression on everyone he encountered. His remarkable talent for winning over his future wife's family solely through his abilities filled his parents with immense pride. Here's how it all went down: Sharda Ben's brother also worked in Kanpur and was closely associated with Mansukh Bhai. He was thoroughly impressed by Mansukh Bhai's dedication, hard work, energy, and enthusiasm for the business. He believed Mansukh Bhai was the perfect groom for his sister and discussed this with his father. He even mentioned that Mansukh Bhai hailed from Narali, a village close to their own in Gujarat. Upon hearing this, Sharda Ben's father sent a marriage proposal for his daughter to the house of Mansukh Bhai's father, Mahadev Bhai. Unsurprisingly, Mansukh Bhai's incredible abilities won him the love and admiration of his future in-laws!

In January 1948, Mahadev Bhai received a marriage proposal for his son. After discussing it with Maniben, he decided to proceed with the proposal and fixed the marriage of his son with Sharda Ben. A telegram was sent to Mansukh Bhai to inform him of the good news. Upon receiving the telegram, Mansukh Bhai felt a surge of energy and motivation. It was unsurprising because he had worked hard for five years and saved an impressive sum of Rs. 5000 through his business. This was a significant achievement as he had only Rs. 14 when he left his village. Apart from this, he was about to embark on a new journey with his soon-to-be wife.

After receiving the telegram, Mansukh Bhai started thinking about returning home to Narali village with the money he had earned. However, he was concerned about what would happen to his business while he was away. He contacted his relatives who lived in Kanpur to help him with his hawking work. They were more than happy to take over his established business, even though it was for a short period. Mansukh Bhai gave them clear instructions. He advised them to never be lazy, never shy away from hard work, and to do their best to avoid hurting customers through bad words.

Additionally, he requested that they keep a complete account of their daily activities and continue to visit the areas where customers used to wait. Finally, he emphasized that trust and honesty were the keys to a successful business. After convincing his relatives, Mansukh Bhai left Kanpur for Narali with the money and many belongings for his parents and siblings.

Lost in old memories...

As the train departed from Kanpur, Mansukh Bhai found himself lost in old memories from 1943 when he had left Narali, hoping to succeed in Kanpur. Over the past few years, Mansukh Bhai had matured beyond his age and had become an expert in dedicating himself to hard work without looking back. When he was coming to Kanpur five years ago, he could only afford to drink tea at two stations due to financial constraints. He had to suppress his desires, but now, five years later, there was a glow of success on his face as he travelled in the super-class.

Mansukh Bhai firmly believed in the dictum: *"Time is definitely cruel, but time also helps those who take bold steps."* He lived by this philosophy, and it brought him tremendous success. When he arrived at Viramgam station in Surendranagar, the sweet fragrance of Kathiawar's soil refreshed him. Five years ago, he had visited this station with his father, but now the conditions at Viramgam station and Mansukh Bhai's circumstances had changed. Mansukh Bhai hired a horse carriage and left with his luggage to go to Narali village.

Upon reaching the village, Mansukh Bhai noticed several changes that had occurred. People greeted him along the way, but he was determined to reach his destination immediately. He met many individuals who used to buy goods from his father's shop, and though they attempted to talk with him, he politely replied and proceeded. Finally, he arrived at his home, kissed the threshold as a sign of his affection for his family and home, and went inside. His mother became emotional and ran towards him as soon as she saw him. They hugged each other, and tears of joy flowed from her eyes. Mansukh Bhai was delighted to be reunited with his family.

After this, he went to his father's shop and touched his father's feet as a sign of respect. However, a customer arrived when he was about to embrace his father. Mahadev Bhai turned towards the customer instead of hugging his son. This was another significant lesson for Mansukh Bhai. His father silently conveyed that *"while relationships and respect are crucial, customers always come first. If you treat your customers like gods, the goddess Lakshmi will never be unhappy, and your reputation will remain intact."*

Mansukh Bhai's unwavering dedication to his family business was truly admirable. When the customer arrived, instead of giving in to the temptation of hugging his father, he opted to help him with the transaction. This selflessness left a lasting impression on Mahadev Bhai, who was thrilled that Mansukh Bhai had remained true to his values over the years. Upon reaching the village, Mansukh Bhai wasted no time in getting to work with his father, prioritizing the business's success over leisure time with his siblings.

When Mansukh Bhai and his father returned home in the evening, everyone eagerly awaited them. Mahadev Bhai asked Mansukh to rest, assuming he must have been tired from the journey. However, Mansukh Bhai was resilient and didn't feel exhausted. He had dinner with his parents and refreshed his memories with his siblings.

Mahadev Bhai inquired about his son's well-being and said, *"Son, I am very happy that you have learned to earn money and become self-sufficient. It is a blessing from our ancestors and the grace of God. I take no credit for this. Remember one thing, family is our biggest asset. The more love and attention you give to your family, the more it will flourish. You know how to earn money, but it's important to use it wisely, continuously increase your capital, bring in new ideas, and spend time with your family at the end of the day. Don't forget to calm your mind by spending time with your loved ones. Family, love, affection, emotions, feelings, and relationships are essential for the growth of your business and building your reputation. Don't be disheartened by any difficulties that come your way. Embrace joy and cherish happy moments."* Mahadev Bhai went on to give his son many other pieces of advice.

He also informed Mansukh Bhai that his marriage had been arranged with Sharda Ben, Premchand's daughter, from the nearby village of Muli.

Mahatma Gandhi's assassination changes the mood

On 30 January 1948, the family gathered to worship their *Kuldevi,* a family goddess. Later, they performed the *haldi* ceremony for Mansukh Bhai. Throughout the night, auspicious songs were sung in the house, and the family hosted a dinner for hundreds of guests. The atmosphere in the village was festive, with lanterns and petromax lit outside all the houses, as there was no electricity in the town until Mansukh Bhai's marriage.

However, the next day, the mood changed drastically due to the news of Mahatma Gandhi's assassination. Although it had happened the day before in the evening, news spread slowly in those days. The sad news reached the village early the next morning. The villagers were filled with grief, but on the advice of other elders, Mahadev Bhai decided to continue with his son's marriage ceremony. Cancelling the wedding programme was considered inauspicious after the *haldi* rituals.

The power of karma

Mansukh Bhai firmly believed in the power of karma and viewed hard work and perseverance as the only means to achieve success and victory. He thought that luck was merely a byproduct of one's karma. Despite returning to his village for his wedding, Mansukh Bhai never took a day off and continued managing his father's shop with unwavering dedication. He was delighted to see the business becoming more profitable. Mansukh Bhai wanted to share his happiness with his loved ones, so he invited all his old acquaintances to his wedding. Bullock carts were arranged for the wedding procession to transport people from the village to the bride's place.

As the sun rose on 1 February 1948, preparations began for the grand occasion. Mansukh Bhai, his father Mahadev Bhai, and others rode beautifully decorated bullock carts to Muli village. The procession arrived before evening and was hosted in public residences nearby. As the sun set, Mansukh Bhai rode a majestic horse to his in-laws' house, where the wedding procession was greeted with a grand welcome at the gate. The ceremony began with pundits reciting *Swasti* and women singing auspicious songs while Mansukh Bhai and Sharda Ben garlanded each other. The wedding was conducted with the mantras of *Saptapadi.* The next day, Sharda Ben's parents gave her an emotional *vidai,* and Mansukh Bhai returned to his house in Narali with his wife, Sharda Ben, who was sitting shyly, wearing a long veil.

After his wedding, Mansukh Bhai began to feel that he needed to shift his focus back to his business. He was contemplating asking his father for permission to return to Kanpur when, one evening, his father suddenly said, "Mansukh, the wedding is over and all the rituals have been completed. Now, you should get back to work." Mansukh Bhai was taken aback by his father's remark, as he had been thinking about the same thing the previous night. He wondered how his father had known what was on his mind. However, he soon realized that his father did not possess the power to read minds. Instead, the importance of hard work, earning money, and using time well had been instilled in his father by his ancestors. These same values had been passed down to Mansukh Bhai by his father.

A valuable lesson from his father: "Manage your money with care."

On 15 February 1948, after marrying Sharda Ben, Mansukh Bhai left for Kanpur. Before leaving, he kept only Rs. 1000 of the remaining money with himself and gave the rest to his siblings, father, and mother. However, his father refused to take the money, *saying that it was hard-earned money and spending it casually would develop a habit of careless spending, which could become dangerous.* Mansukh Bhai did not take the money back from his father but remembered this lesson as an essential part of his life.

Mansukh Bhai and his wife, Sharda Ben, arrived in a bullock cart at the station. Mansukh's father wanted to remind him of his responsibilities, so he said, "Until now, you were alone, but now you have someone else to take care of. Always remember this." He also advised him, "Work hard, but don't let our daughter-in-law suffer. Try to return home every evening and spend time with her. Don't worry about us at all." Mahadev Bhai smiled, "Now spend the money carefully as per your wish." Just then, the train whistled, and Mansukh Bhai touched his father's feet, took his blessings, and boarded the train.

Upon arriving in Kanpur with her husband, Sharda Ben was immensely thrilled. She was eager to explore the city and catch up with some family members. Even before getting married, she had always been fascinated with Kanpur. Although the train journey had been tiring, Mansukh Bhai took Sharda Ben to his rented house as soon as they arrived. Sharda Ben immediately started cleaning the house enthusiastically; her energy was contagious. She then cooked a delicious dinner with passion. Mansukh Bhai went to bed that night, excitedly planning his hawking business, which he was to resume the following day.

The newlywed couple had high hopes and dreams for their future together, but *something else was in store.* The very next day, Mansukh Bhai suffered an unimaginable setback. However, Sharda Ben provided unwavering support and comfort during this difficult time, and her steadfast devotion to her partner continued throughout their lives together. Sharda Ben was not just Mansukh Bhai's life partner but also his equal business partner. In the 1950s, when the term 'women's empowerment' was unknown, Mansukh Bhai set a perfect example.

SECTION 2

"Character cannot be developed in ease and quiet. Only through experience of trial and suffering can the soul be strengthened, ambition inspired and success achieved."

– Helen Keller, American Author, Disability Rights Advocate

8

Life at a Crossroads Again

"It feels strange to know that today no matter what
Even if it happens, the sun will come out again
tomorrow."

– *Aaron Lauritsen, Author*

Imagine a young man who had recently gotten married. He was eager to return to work and take care of his business. However, on his first day, he received shocking news. His close and trusted relatives had betrayed him, leaving him at a crossroads. Can you imagine being in such a situation? It's easy to feel defeated in such adversity, but Mansukh Bhai was not one to bow down. He refused to give up or let others dictate his destiny. If you were in his shoes, what would you do? Remember, success isn't just about avoiding failures; it's also about bouncing back from them. Mansukh Bhai's only mistake was trusting his close relatives too much. Betrayal is not always easy to recognize. One scholar wisely said, "*You should not pay attention to the betrayal you can see. The truly terrible betrayal is the one that remains completely hidden from your eyes.*" This is a lesson that Mansukh Bhai learned the hard way.

After reaching Kanpur, Mansukh Bhai met with his relatives who had been taking care of the hawking business. They informed him that there was a 'loss' in the business. Mansukh Bhai had never heard the word 'loss' before. He used to buy goods from shops on credit, sell them, and easily keep the profit. However, he was surprised to hear about the loss as he had yet to be given a satisfactory answer as to where the goods or the earnings had gone. After four days of investigation, he realized that his relatives had been discussing 'losses' to remove him from the business. At this stage, Mansukh Bhai made a tough decision to separate himself from these relatives in business. The relatives were happy because their plan had worked. The belongings were divided after parting ways with relatives, but the relatives were dishonest. Although Mansukh Bhai should have received Rs. 800 when the cost was divided, the relatives only gave him Rs. 400. Despite this setback, Mansukh Bhai did not let it discourage him but instead took it as a challenge. He chose to view the insult as an opportunity for growth rather than seeking revenge. *History has shown that those who improve themselves after experiencing an insult often achieve remarkable results.*

Mansukh Bhai found himself at a crossroads in his life after he was betrayed in his small business. He had two options - he could either seek revenge and spend all his energy on recovering the money his relatives had withheld from him, or he could forget the past and focus on achieving new goals for success. Mansukh Bhai decided his relationships were more important than money and didn't want to risk losing them. Therefore, he embarked on a new journey and worked even harder to earn more money. This decision was right, as he could achieve his goals and maintain his relationships simultaneously.

Mansukh Bhai had gained a good reputation among businessmen in Kanpur due to his valuable experience. His reputation was so strong that no amount of betrayal could take it away from him. One day, he proposed to a businessman that he could bring cosmetic items from Calcutta at discounted rates, and the businessman happily accepted his proposal. Along with the cosmetic items, Mansukh Bhai started bringing toffees, biscuits, and other items from Calcutta for himself. Before getting married, he would only travel to nearby towns, but after marriage, he decided to explore deeper into the villages. His hawking goods were sold out within two days in the towns around Kanpur, and small traders from many villages even made him promise to bring more goods soon. Through this experience, Mansukh Bhai learned that there were business opportunities not only in the cities but also in villages.

No rest for six months!

Mansukh Bhai's relentless work ethic and business dedication were remarkable. After starting again, for the next six months, he tirelessly travelled to different villages, hawking goods without taking a day of rest. His perseverance and hard work paid off, as he turned his initial investment of Rs. 400 into a sum of Rs. 2000, which was considered impressive in those days. Throughout this time, his wife, Sharda Ben, stood by his side, supporting him in every way possible. Despite her privileged upbringing, Sharda Ben was inspired by her husband's unwavering commitment to his work and his passion for success. She helped him by preparing bags, cooking meals, and managing household chores while he was away. In fact, she even found time to sew and weave after her daily prayers. Sharda Ben's constant encouragement and support motivated Mansukh Bhai to push himself harder.

Learned the art of investment very quickly...

After rapidly mastering the art of investment, Mansukh Bhai's income increased over the next few months. He utilized his savings of Rs. 2000 to acquire the agency of Sathe biscuits, which had just been introduced to the market. Mansukh Bhai worked tirelessly to promote Sathe biscuits and boost its sales. His wife, Sharda Ben, also played a crucial role in selling Sathe biscuits. Despite managing all household chores, Sharda Ben would help by packing the biscuits into bags and hanging them on Mansukh Bhai's bicycle. Even though they lived in a one-room house, she never complained but always prayed for his excellent health so that he could continue working hard and earning money honestly. Mansukh Bhai continued to sell Sathe biscuits, going to fairs and festivals, and returning only after selling all the biscuits in both bags. Through his efforts, Sathe biscuits became the preferred choice of the people and shopkeepers. In the meantime, on 12 October 1949, they were blessed with a son who was named Vikram.

Mansukh Bhai was a man of great wisdom and prudence. When his son Vikram was born, he faced financial difficulties. However, he remained focused and spent only within his means. His love for his wife and family was unwavering, and he worked tirelessly day and night to ensure their well-being.

Unlike others, Mansukh Bhai invested his hard-earned savings wisely. He knew the value of saving and had learned this skill over time. He even took out a life insurance policy in his and his wife's name, not for their old age, but in case they faced any difficult times. He believed the investment would be safe in the government treasury if the policy was not used. *In modern times, investing and reinvesting are common. Mansukh Bhai learned this skill in an era when people slept with seven locks on their safes and the keys tied around their waists.*

Amid his business pursuits, Mansukh Bhai found solace in the joy brought to him by his growing family. With the arrival of his second son, Deepak Bhai, and Goddess Laxmi-like daughter, Rita, the laughter of three children filled the entire courtyard of their home. Though Mansukh Bhai was content with the happiness his family brought him, he still yearned for more tremendous success in his business. Despite the business running smoothly, his drive to achieve new heights of success only intensified. With the happiness of his family as his motivation, Mansukh Bhai was determined to make his business thrive.

A quick learner

Mansukh Bhai worked harder with each passing day. After receiving an offer from Sathe Biscuit Company, he became the distributor of Sathe Biscuits in Kanpur. With his hard work, dedication, and energy, Mansukh Bhai made Sathe Biscuits popular in both districts, Kanpur and Lucknow, and the rural areas. He took Sathe Biscuits to new heights that the company never even imagined. While selling Sathe Biscuits, he learned that the game of biscuits lasts only a few days, and they must be kept for a short time. He also knew it was better to buy new goods only after they were sold because biscuits started changing colour after two months, and their oil started coming off. In those days, paper packaging was used. While selling Sathe Biscuits, he learned every detail about the industry, from biscuit manufacturing, raw material, and packing to distribution and returns. *Being a quick learner, Mansukh Bhai never needed to memorize anything; he quickly learned the details by watching the process of something in one go.*

Mansukh Bhai was a true inspiration to everyone who knew him. His unrelenting drive and passion for work had become his defining traits. He always aimed to take his business to new heights, but as his children grew up, he realized that his aspirations were far greater than just Sathe Biscuits. With God's help, he was prepared for a new challenge – to expand his business and continuously sell new products. Mansukh Bhai's efficiency, hard work, and ability to anticipate market trends and identify buyers earned him a stellar reputation in the business world of these districts.

Never learned to accept defeat...

Mansukh Bhai believed that success could only be achieved through hard work and persistence. Even in the most challenging circumstances, he refused to give up. He did not lose hope when his relatives left him with only a meagre amount of capital. Instead, he sought opportunities to improve his situation, knowing that life can be unpredictable and change for the better. Mansukh Bhai used to say to himself, *"Circumstances keep changing in life. My days will also change. Although there may be a shortage of money now, a day will come when it will be difficult to count the money."*

Mansukh Bhai once said, *"Hard work and efficiency don't need a mirror or noise to impress anyone."* His diverse work experience included counting bricks, selling goods in Kanpur and Lucknow, and procuring goods from Calcutta. This had taught him excellence that speaks for itself. He firmly believed that one need not boast about one's work if it's exceptional.

By 1959, India had been independent for 12 years, and Pandit Jawaharlal Nehru, the country's first Prime Minister, shared a message that still holds true today. He emphasized that success favours those who are willing to take bold action and face the consequences of their decisions instead of those who hesitate. Mansukh Bhai was inspired by Nehru's words and decided to be bold. He knew that great rewards awaited those who seized opportunities.

A young Mansukh Bhai Kothari.

Mansukh Bhai with his son, Deepak.

Mansukh Bhai graciously attending a community event hosted in his native village, Narali, in Gujarat.

Mansukh Bhai and Deepak (left) during the inauguration of the Kothari International School.

Deepak and family enjoying quality time together.

9

Evolving into a Savvy Businessman

"To be successful, you have to have your heart in your business, and your business in your heart."

– Thomas Watson, Sr., Former CEO, IBM

By 1959, Mansukh Bhai had already devoted more than a decade to tireless business work. Thanks to his remarkable ability to quickly grasp business intricacies, he established a unique identity in the field. Businessmen started acknowledging his business acumen, and his success began to soar. By 34, Mansukh Bhai had an impressive business profile that would make any professional envious even today. Through tremendous hard work, he had become a savvy businessman, so it was only natural that big success would soon knock on his door.

In early 1959, the East India Company of Madras hired Mansukh Bhai for his exceptional marketing skills. He was renowned for his efficiency, hard work, and talent in identifying potential customers and business opportunities in untapped markets. Additionally, he had a remarkable ability to learn quickly. The company offered him a job to market bath soap, and he accepted it, but he made it clear to the company that he would only work on a commission basis and devise his own marketing strategy. Meanwhile, a businessman from Kanpur had secured the OK Soap distributorship but needed assistance in making the soap popular in Uttar Pradesh and Bihar. As the newly appointed marketer for OK Soap, Mansukh Bhai started working in Kanpur. Within a few months, he successfully made OK Soap a household name in Kanpur, which ultimately benefited the distributor. During a meeting in Madras, the OK Soap distributor from Kanpur introduced Mansukh Bhai's name to the company's other distributors and management. Mansukh Bhai worked tirelessly in various jobs, from counting bricks to selling goods.

Mansukh Bhai was a brave individual who constantly sought new challenges and opportunities. Even when he had established a sense of comfort in his current position, he was always looking for something new to explore. One such opportunity presented itself when he was offered a job promoting OK Bath Soap for the East India Company of Madras in Patna. This marked a significant second turning point in his life.

Upon hearing the Kanpur distributor's words during a meeting in Madras, the management of the East India Company decided to meet Mansukh Bhai in person. However, for some reason, this was not possible. It turned out that the situation was more complicated than it seemed. When the company could not contact Mansukh Bhai, they asked their Kanpur distributor to send him to Patna. Initially, the distributor was concerned about his business in Kanpur. Still, since it was the company's order, he called Mansukh Bhai, explained the situation, and informed him about the offer to go to Patna. The news of receiving an offer from a big company made Mansukh Bhai ecstatic. This was the first time he had received such an offer from a company. It was a testament to Mansukh Bhai's relentless hard work, dedication, and integrity that the company's management, which he had only heard of, knew him by name and was highly impressed by his work. Upon hearing about the offer from the distributor, Mansukh Bhai asked for some time to think and went home.

Initially, Mansukh Bhai was always preoccupied with business issues, leaving little time for the family; however, knowing the situation, his wife, Sharda Ben, did not complain or discuss the matter with him. While facing these challenges, Mansukh Bhai had a detailed discussion about OK Soap at home with his wife. He did not want to leave his family in Kanpur but thought it was not feasible to take them to Bihar as it could adversely affect his other business. Sharda Ben was a supportive life partner and said, "You have a well-established business, and people know and recognize you. Maybe God has given you this opportunity to change the situation. There is no problem at home in Kanpur. I will take care of the children and try my best to assist you with your work as a friend. We also have acquaintances in the city, so don't worry. Maybe OK Soap will change our fortunes, and even if it doesn't, the experience you gain may open up new business opportunities. My conscience tells me that you will be successful by going there. I will handle all the household work. You go there with a relaxed mind without worrying about anything."

Mansukh Bhai decided to travel to Patna after his wife encouraged him. He realized that he would not have to bear the burden of investing in OK Soap as he only needed to transport goods from Kanpur to Bihar, sell them, and seek the assistance of agents to help with their sale. Additionally, he knew he needed to promote the product in a new and innovative way. His excitement increased twofold after receiving his wife's approval. Consequently, he temporarily left his established Sathe Biscuits business in Kanpur and Lucknow to venture into Bihar. Within two days, he cleared the remaining stock of Sathe biscuits. After consulting with the OK Soap distributor, he proceeded on his journey to Patna.

Patna was a new place for him. The distributor trusted him and gave him Rs. 200. He stayed in a hotel for Rs. 15 per day and surveyed the city on foot and by rickshaw, talking to wholesalers and retailers in many markets. Despite being a stranger, people listened attentively to Mansukh Bhai. This resulted from his adept negotiation skills, ability to diversify and expand business into new markets, innovative business strategies, and talent for persuading fellow businessmen. He convinced 10-12 people to sell the soap and, after five days, returned to Kanpur to collect the goods for OK Soap.

Mansukh Bhai's formulas were unique...

He took the goods on his credit from the OK Soap distributor in Kanpur. He again left for Patna with the goods. In a short period of just one year in Patna, he not only made OK Soap popular but also took it to new heights of sales. The company officials invited Mansukh Bhai to a meeting in Madras to honour him for his work. The company discussed the business strategies of Mansukh Bhai. One of the company's directors spoke onstage, "The formulas of doing business that Mansukh Bhai knows, he did not even study them in England. Mansukh Bhai is an amazing personality." After this, the company itself took the initiative and offered Mansukh Bhai the agency of OK Soap in Kanpur. This was the first time that Mansukh Bhai had talked to the top officers of a company. Mansukh Bhai learned that hard work speaks for itself, so he happily accepted the company's offer.

He needed more money for the company's agency, and the opportunity was knocking on his door. He did not understand what to do, but Mansukh Bhai did not despair. He remembered lines from the famous poet Maithili Sharan Gupta's poem, which he had heard somewhere, "*Be a man, don't let your mind down, do some work, do some work, live in the world and make some name.*" Even amidst stress, Mansukh Bhai found a new path for himself. He surrenderd the insurance policy under his and his wife's name and founded Sharda Traders in 1959. He secured the distributorship of OK Soap. Working hard day and night, he campaigned in the entire city, sometimes by bicycle, sometimes on foot, and sometimes in a vehicle. He met and talked to people continuously. He enumerated the virtues of the soap and promised a continuous supply. The result was in his favour. OK Soap was visible in almost every shop of the city in just four months. Many people were buying it. Within six months, OK Soap reached the number one spot in the market in Kanpur city.

Hawk-eyed, always looking out for new business ideas

After success with his soap business, Mansukh Bhai kept his eyes open for new business opportunities. During a visit to Madras, he found an Amla oil bottle in his hotel bathroom and realized that such a product was unavailable in Kanpur. This gave him the idea for an Amla oil startup. In 1959, he launched his homemade Amla oil under the brand name *Jyoti Brahmi Amla oil,* quickly becoming popular in the market.

Despite his success, he remained focused on his family's future. In 1961, he used some of the money he had earned to invest in his younger son Deepak Bhai Kothari's education and sent him out of Kanpur to study. He believed that education was an investment that would pay off in the long run and could not be purchased later.

Mansukh Bhai continued to run his soap and Amla oil businesses for the next five years while exploring other opportunities.

Revives a sinking company...

In 1964, Mansukh Bhai invested a significant part of his earnings from OK Soap in *Chhota Bhai Beedi Company*, a company in Kanpur that belonged to his friend and was on the verge of collapsing. Instead of living a life of luxury, he decided to take a risk and revive the sinking company.

To promote *Chhota Bhai Beedi,* Mansukh Bhai had frequent meetings with the distributor partners of OK Soap, which resulted in positive outcomes. Within a year, the *Beedi* company started earning profits, although in small amounts initially. Mansukh Bhai remained a partner with that company for a long time, successfully bringing it back from the brink of failure.

Not afraid of taking risks in business...

Mansukh Bhai was a fearless entrepreneur who ran multiple businesses simultaneously. Although investing in various ventures was risky, he enjoyed taking risks, overcoming challenges, and achieving success. Among his businesses were OK Soap, Jyoti Brahmi Amla Oil, and Chhota Bhai Beedi. Mansukh Bhai worked tirelessly every day to grow his businesses and take the market to new heights.

After accumulating wealth, Mansukh Bhai started his own industry in a rented one-room house. Despite the small space, he decided not to change the house. His wife, Sharda Ben, was his biggest supporter and helped him with every aspect of his business while caring for the household and raising their children. Mansukh Bhai credited her for his success, saying, *"My life partner has made the most significant contribution to my success. If you consider your wife as your ally, success is sure."*

Mansukh Bhai founded *Kothari Chemicals* in 1965. He also sold Jyoti Brahmi Amla oil, biscuits, soap, and Beedi. While doing the Amla oil business, he realized that people prefer coconut oil over amla oil because it's more cost-effective and sells more. After studying the market trends and gaining knowledge from his previous venture, he opened a startup called 'Project Coconut Oil.' He already had the necessary machines and packing material; all he needed was the raw materials.

In 1965, Mansukh Bhai started producing Seven Up coconut oil on a small scale with the help of his wife, Sharda Ben. His trader friends offered him coconuts on credit and helped him arrange for bottles. Mansukh Bhai had been in the business for two decades and had made countless companions among businessmen. He contacted famous Bollywood actress Hema Malini through his Mumbai friends to promote Seven Up. She agreed to do an advertisement in which her graceful and silky hair captured people's attention. As a result, Seven Up coconut oil became an instant hit in the market. Although the sale of Seven Up oil was not as successful as Mansukh Bhai expected, he was not discouraged by it.

Mansukh Bhai acquired valuable experience in product promotion and marketing by introducing Seven Up in the market. He learned various techniques such as putting up posters and banners, maintaining old business contacts, campaigning by installing loudspeakers in rickshaws, and practising public relations. Despite the challenges, he decided to continue with independent business because it offered a better experience than selling someone else's goods. Mansukh Bhai learned from his experience with Seven Up that selling a new product in the market can be challenging, but it's still possible with sufficient time and effort in the right direction.

The joy of buying his first car and then...

In late 1966, Mansukh Bhai fulfilled his dream of buying a new, shiny Fiat car for himself and his family after years of hard work and steadily increasing income. Owning a car at that time was a noteworthy accomplishment as it greatly enhanced his work productivity. As a result of his success and the popularity of Sathe biscuits, Parle biscuit manufacturing company offered him an agency for distribution in Kanpur in 1969. Although Parle was a bigger brand than Sathe Biscuits, Mansukh Bhai also focused on his startup's products, including Seven Up with Sathe Biscuits and OK Soap, and required more funds to buy a Parle agency. The proposal presented a dilemma: invest in an established business or start a new one. After careful consideration, he decided to go with the Parle agency, even if it meant facing financial difficulties. Mansukh Bhai was a visionary and had sensed the potential in Parle.

After making the decision, Mansukh Bhai promptly sold his brand-new Fiat car. While others might have taken out a loan to invest in Parle, Mansukh Bhai had his own principles in business. He knew the car could be repurchased, but the opportunity to invest in Parle might never return. So, he sold the vehicle without any attachment and used the money to purchase a Parle agency. Parle was also waiting for Mansukh Bhai in Kanpur, and it became a hit in the market in no time due to Mansukh Bhai's credibility and efficient business style. He ensured timely availability of goods and guaranteed returns in case of faulty goods. Being very busy, he stopped working on Sathe Biscuits after his stock ran out. Along with Parle, Mansukh Bhai's home industry products were also gaining popularity. As soon as he had enough income, he repurchased the car in 1971.

Belief in equitable distribution

Mansukh Bhai believed in equitable distribution. He invested in his friend's Beedi company and used his business skills to improve its financial health. However, he was committed to fair distribution and ensured that the original owner received only what was agreed upon. Mansukh Bhai wanted to revive the company without exploiting anyone's property. Therefore, he proposed that they split the profits equally, which would benefit both parties.

Mansukh Bhai was associated with many products, so he established *Kothari Sales Corporation* to handle all business in one company and ensure accurate financial accounting. The company's primary objective was to facilitate the business of Seven Up Coconut Oil and Parle Biscuits. This included marketing, tax, inflow of goods, consumption, bringing raw materials, and taking money for the goods sold in the market. The company would also handle publicity to make it easier for the business to run smoothly.

10

The Invention of a Unique Brand – Pan Parag

"The best way to predict the future is to invent it."

– *Alan Curtis, American Computer Scientist*

Success is not an overnight phenomenon but a journey that requires time, effort, and an unwavering commitment to improvement. This is a lesson that Mansukh Bhai learned firsthand during his three-decade-long journey since leaving his village. Despite achieving immense success and wealth, he remained grounded, focused on growing his business, and positively impacting the world. Mansukh Bhai believed that success is not measured by material possessions but by the satisfaction of achieving your goals. His dedication and commitment to excellence were about to propel him to the pinnacle of success that he truly deserved.

Seeds of ultimate success...

The owner of the house where Mansukh Bhai and Baa were living on rent was a Marwari. He used to make a mixture of betel nut, catechu, and cloves at his home, which he mixed with tobacco and consumed. Although Mansukh Bhai and Baa witnessed the landlord doing this many times, they didn't realize that the secret to their ultimate success was right in their house.

One incident that changed it all and scripted history...

One day, an incident occurred that changed everything and made history. Mansukh Bhai visited a crowded *pan* shop and asked the shopkeeper for a cigarette. However, the shopkeeper was busy serving *pan* to regular customers while they discussed various topics. These customers usually bought only one *pan* but requested two to four to take home because they were fond of the unique flavours of that specific shop. Meanwhile, those who purchased cigarettes and beedis had no particular preference for any shop. Mansukh Bhai felt upset when the shopkeeper ignored him. Despite this, he tactfully but firmly asked for a cigarette again, using a slightly louder voice than usual. The shopkeeper gave him the cigarette, but it seemed he was doing him a favour. Mansukh Bhai took it and left for home, pondering something in his mind. This incident had hurt him deeply, but he managed to control his anger. Suddenly, Babuji got an idea. He was an extraordinary person, and his mind worked in unique ways. He took inspiration from the incident at the shop, a crucial step towards his ultimate success.

He arrived home and poured his heart out to his wife, Sharda Ben.

Mansukh Bhai said, "Listen... what if we create an alternative to *pan*?"

Sharda Ben was taken aback. "What? An alternative to *pan*? I don't understand," she replied.

Once again, Sharda Ben returned the responsibility to her husband, placing the ball in his court.

Mansukh Bhai narrated the incident to Baa and suggested that they devise a substitute for *pan,* regardless of the outcome. He expressed his hope that if they could succeed in making an alternative to *pan,* it would significantly impact their lives. Sharda Ben, who had faced many challenges, supported her husband's idea. However, they were faced with several questions: what could be a viable replacement for *pan,* and how could they produce it? More importantly, would *pan* lovers accept the new option? And where would they get the funds to make the *pan* substitute?

Mansukh Bhai and his wife believed in achieving the impossible. They worked tirelessly on various tests to create a formula that became a hit. The couple knew that a great story makes for a great film. Similarly, they believed that a fantastic product like their *pan masala,* which could be carried in one's pocket, eaten anywhere, and last for months, was bound to become an instant success. Mansukh Bhai knew that dreaming was easy, but achieving those dreams required hard work and dedication. He put all his life experience into creating the perfect pan masala and worked day and night towards it. The *third turning point* came when he started *Pan Parag,* which met with huge success.

It took months of hard work to develop the perfect formula, but it became a hit, was used to welcome wedding processions, and became a staple at gatherings. But the *Pan Parag* story is more complex than it seems. Creating this tradition and discovering its unique taste took a long time. This kind of process requires hard work, determination, and many failures. Mansukh Bhai, the inventor of *Pan Parag,* was no exception. He was inspired by great personalities like Newton and believed he would achieve success and recognition one day. He always believed that he would overcome obstacles and succeed. He never let his fears stop him from trying. He believed that time would eventually turn in his favour and his life would improve.

Knew that time would become the most valuable resource!

Mansukh Bhai had a visionary idea to create a ready-made *pan* to save people's time. He believed that time would become the most valuable resource in the future. However, he could never have imagined that this idea would eventually become the foundation of the *pan masala* industry and a popular option for *pan* lovers.

Mansukh Bhai initially hesitated to share his idea because he still had to determine how people would react. He was worried that his idea might not be taken seriously or that people might make fun of him. At the time, people were familiar with 'Mainpuri tobacco' or 'Mainpuri' for its beautiful fragrance. The mixture was kept on brass plates covered with red cloth in small shops at the Ghantaghar intersection to preserve its aroma and specialty. People would buy the mix, add lime, and eat it, but they had to take the betel leaf and lime separately.

Creating an alternative to *pan* was not easy

Mansukh Bhai was passionate about finding an alternative to *pan,* so much so that he often suffered sleepless nights. One night, he woke up feeling restless and unable to sleep. His desire to find a solution consumed him once again. He tried to calm himself by walking restlessly, but when that failed, he woke his wife up and asked for her help.

He explained his dilemma to her and expressed his determination to start working on the alternative the next day. However, his wife was not too pleased about being woken up in the middle of the night. She tried calming him down by telling him it was too late and that they could discuss it in the morning.

When Baa woke up in the morning, she was surprised that Mansukh Bhai had already bathed and gotten ready. Mansukh Bhai couldn't sleep at night because he kept thinking about *pan* seller's shop and the possible alternative to *pan.* When *Baa* suggested he go to the market to buy some things, Mansukh Bhai was surprised and asked which things she meant. He clarified that they already had catechu, betel nut, a pliers set, and chunauti (a box for keeping lime) at home, so they could start making the mixture. Mansukh Bhai talked about it in a childlike manner.

Baa told Mansukh Bhai that making the mixture was challenging. She questioned him about how he would make it since he smoked cigarettes and never prepared a *pan.* Baa pointed out that he had never even cut betel nuts and cloves before and only knew how to eat *pan.* Mansukh Bhai acknowledged that his wife was right, but he interrupted her and said there was no need to argue. He asked Baa if she knew how to make it, and she said she would do it. However, he was determined to make the mixture, no matter what. Baa understood her husband's passion and knew it was impossible to stop him once he had decided something. The next day, the couple began to work on an alternative to *pan.* They started making the mixture only in the morning, and Mansukh Bhai would leave the house for his other work, telling Baa to make it. When he returned home at night, he would ask about the mixture first and then sit down to eat.

As Mansukh Bhai was fond of eating *pan* and smoking cigarettes, he already had all the necessary ingredients for the alternative to *pan* in his cupboard. However, it was a different matter that only Baa used to prepare *pan,* while Mansukh Bhai only knew to eat it. In fact, the tradition of keeping *pandan* in Indian culture dates back centuries. Elders used to keep a silver *pandan,* which contained betel nut, catechu, clove, cardamom, and nutmeg. A similar arrangement was also present at Mansukh Bhai's house. They started making a powder of all the essential things one by one, often experimenting with different mixtures of cloves, cardamom, betel leaves, betel nuts, catechu, etc. The happiness on their faces was worth seeing as they made the mixture. Mansukh Bhai's heart brimmed with pure joy, as if he was on the verge of uncovering a priceless treasure. They did this work many times, but they were yet to achieve the desired success.

Mansukh Bhai and his wife would work on perfecting their *pan* substitute mixture after a tiring workday. They faced many challenges, from lack of taste to excessive moisture. Despite the setbacks, Mansukh Bhai's family supported his new home industry, now known as a 'startup'. While Mansukh Bhai worked during the day, he spent his nights searching for the missing ingredient that would make their mixture unique. His family also helped in various ways, such as preparing the mixture and performing other related tasks. Despite not knowing how long it would take, they all worked together towards success. Mansukh Bhai and his wife never gave up, and their unity indicated they were getting closer to achieving their dream goal.

An exciting search for the appropriate fragrance

Mansukh Bhai embarked on an exciting search for fragrance. During his search, he discovered that 'Mainpuri' also has its own unique fragrance. One day, he went to Ghantaghar to meet the seller of the Mainpuri mixture and inquired, "Brother, could you tell me where the fragrance in this mixture comes from? How do you mix it? Or does it come mixed?" The Mainpuri seller's response to Mansukh Bhai's query about the source of the fragrance was rather ambiguous. Instead of giving a straightforward answer, he vaguely mentioned that it comes from Kannauj. This prompted Mansukh Bhai to decide to go to Kannauj and bring the best fragrance. He informed Baa that evening, "Listen, I will be going to Kannauj tomorrow." Before he could finish his sentence, Baa asked, "Why? Why Kannauj?"

Mansukh Bhai replied, "There should be a fragrance in our mixture. You know that the *pan* seller adds many types of fragrances, and the Mainpuri seller also adds fragrances. That fragrance is available in Kannauj, which is the city of perfumes. I will go there and bring the best fragrance. We can then see if our mixture is a hit."

Enthusiastic and happy, he shared his plans with Baa. She knew he was stubborn and determined to do whatever he wanted, so she agreed to his proposal.

The next day, Mansukh Bhai abandoned all his work and headed to Kannauj in search of fragrances. He visited numerous shops and conversed with several people, hoping to find the right scent. He even spoke to a few *pan* sellers, but he needed to gain more knowledge on the subject. Whenever Mansukh Bhai faced a dilemma or did not understand something, he would recall his father's advice. His father had told him to compare the most expensive and the cheapest options, examine the quality, and trust his instincts. Mansukh Bhai needed help figuring out where to begin with this task. However, he possessed an extraordinary sense of smell, which he often boasted about. He would say, "I can detect even the slightest fragrance instantly." Even Baa was impressed with his nose.

Mansukh Bhai spent a significant amount of time searching for the perfect fragrance. He went to numerous shops before discovering a delightful scent that caught his interest. He visited a perfume shop to learn more about the fragrance and asked the shopkeeper about its uses and the differences between using it as a perfume and consuming it. The shopkeeper explained the nuances in great detail, which impressed Mansukh Bhai. He then asked to see their most special perfume and tried several before finding the one he had been looking for. He returned home to Kanpur with his prized possession, a magical perfume, and shared his discovery with his wife. He urged her to blend it with their mix to experience its wonders.

He added some perfume from Kannauj to his mixture and tasted it himself. He was thrilled with the taste and asked Baa to try it. She too liked the mixture, so Mansukh Bhai was satisfied with his choice. He added fragrance to his mixture for the first time, and everyone praised it when he gave it to his acquaintances. This boosted his morale. After a long struggle, he finally created a delicious *pan masala* formula with a good mixture and aroma. After trying it, Mansukh Bhai and Baa would prepare to pack it and take it to the market. However, they were still afraid of the market, even after having prepared a satisfactory recipe. Would the market accept anything new? How would it be sold? Would people like it or not? Mansukh Bhai was an expert market player, so he knew the nuances of the market very well, but he was still considering every aspect.

Initially distributed packets for free

Mansukh Bhai tested the market for his new recipe as an alternative to the *pan* by initially distributing some packets in the shops, free of charge. Unfortunately, all the shopkeepers rejected his recipe, which disheartened him. Despite this setback, Mansukh Bhai persevered and continued experimenting with new formulas. He frequently visited the perfume city of Kannauj to search for better fragrances and brought back Kewra liquid with sandalwood and rose to mix them and taste the flavours. When satisfied with the taste, he would start packaging the recipe. He worked on his recipes and packaging all night long, and during the day, he would give away some packets for free and sell the rest at various *pan* shops. But the result was always the same. Despite the lack of success, Mansukh Bhai did not lose hope and kept putting in his best effort.

Babuji strongly believed – *success can only be achieved through a small opening, but the possibilities are vast once inside. To enter, one must work hard and be patient.* With this conviction, he continued working towards his goals. For many days, he tried selling his *pan* mixture in several shops but wasn't receiving any positive response from anywhere. Despite not receiving big orders or encouragement from shopkeepers, he refused to accept defeat. The shopkeepers informed him there was no market demand for his product, but Mansukh Bhai remained determined to achieve his objectives.

Mansukh Bhai had been working on his 'dream project' for a long time. He spent many days and nights preparing a ready-made *pan masala* mixture, which he gave away for free. He also spent his savings on this project. The situation eventually got to the point where he considered taking a loan. Still, he always stopped short of doing so, given the indifference of those close to him, his family responsibilities, and his moral values.

One night, around midnight, he suddenly woke up and started walking as if it were morning. He mumbled to himself as if he had a flood of thoughts. He wondered where he was going wrong, if he was on the right path, and what would happen if he failed. Would people make fun of him?

Mansukh Bhai was trapped in a whirlpool of thoughts and had begun to doubt his idea. Baa had woken up due to the noise and looked at her husband. At that time, he was interested in something other than the *pan masala* items or the work of mixing and packing, which was unusual. Babuji was very worried about his dream project. He wanted to do something bigger, and his dream had to be realized somehow. Mansukh Bhai's struggle was two-sided - on the one hand, he fought for his product, and on the other, he fought to drive away depressing and contrary thoughts. He decided to continue working on his product, rejecting all the negativity within him. He was firm on his decision to take his project forward and heard a voice from within telling him that he was on the right track and would be successful. By muttering similar words, Mansukh Bhai strengthened and consoled himself, and his facial expressions changed.

A project that turned into a passion

Babuji faced initial financial losses, but discovered his dream project could also become his passion. He firmly believed—*where there is a will, there is a way,* and he turned every negative thought or disappointment into an opportunity to learn and grow. These thoughts became his daily mantras. Gradually, his unique product gained popularity in the market, and Babuji stopped giving it away for free and began selling it.

Babuji often joked with his friends that *success does not come easy, nor is it inherited. He added that success becomes challenging when people feel tired and doubt their work. However, when a person throws these negative thoughts out and believes they are just a few steps away from success, the destination becomes desperate to kiss their feet.*

He started visiting *pan* shops with a newfound enthusiasm and energy. Every day, he would tell the shopkeepers that his *pan masala* was unique in taste and aroma and would provide a 'new freshness' to their lives if they tried it. He firmly believed in his product and conveyed the same message to his customers and the shopkeepers. This incredible moment led to the creation of a legendary brand. Despite facing numerous challenges and obstacles, he persevered and eventually achieved great success. He had reached a 'new dawn', and the future looked bright. In fact, the dawn was so beautiful that it inspired him to exclaim, *"Dhoom Macha De, Rang Jama De!"*

He used to say, "*During difficult times in life, when we feel helpless and unsuccessful, it's important to keep our emotions in check and be polite to our team and loved ones. They are our real strength." It's said that the darker the night of struggle, the brighter the sun of success shines.* This proved to be true in Babuji's life. The truth dawned on him when he received his first order from a local shop for the *pan masala* he had made. A shopkeeper said, "Mansukh Bhai, please supply the *pudiya*. Many people have come asking for it, and some have even asked who makes it. There is a demand for your mixture, so please make at least 20-25 *pudiyas* and deliver them tomorrow. It's not right if the customers return empty-handed."

Mansukh Bhai listened carefully to each word. After many days and nights of hard work, these were the words he had been yearning to hear. When he received his first order, he smiled like a child deep inside, even though he remained outwardly serious in front of the shopkeeper. His happiness knew no bounds. He immediately ran home and shared the good news with his better half, who supported him every step of the way.

Mansukh Bhai excitedly called his wife, asking her to come quickly as there was a demand for their mixture. Busy with household chores, Baa immediately left everything and came to him. Mansukh Bhai went to get the necessary ingredients while Baa gathered everything they needed to make the mixture. Though they made *pan masala* together daily and gave it to the *pan* shops for free, today was different as they had to make 20 *pudiyas* in half a day. While they were working, Baa asked a question that was on her mind.

"What will be the price of our unique product?"

Mansukh Bhai, the product's creator, had not determined its cost. However, after careful consideration, he proposed a plan that would benefit both the shopkeepers and himself. To assess customer demand, they would initially sell the product at a slightly lower cost, similar to Mainpuri *pudiya*. This would help them to set a final price later. Mansukh Bhai then took the finished product to the *pan* seller and mentioned the proposed price.

Mansukh Bhai was determined to create a unique and exceptional product that would stand out in the market. He spent numerous sleepless nights perfecting the taste and aroma of his *pan masala* and ensuring it was always available. He was attentive to the demand and ensured enough supply to meet it. Although he only provided a small amount of *pan masala,* he always aimed to enhance its quality. As he delved into the intricacies of price and quantity, his mind became occupied with multiple challenges. To overcome them, he sought the counsel of Baa, who had played a pivotal role in his product's success. Together, they deliberated strategies to ensure maximum customer satisfaction while maintaining profitability.

How 'Pan Parag' was named...

The story behind the name of 'Pan Parag' goes like this. The mixture had already been produced and was being sold in the market, but the question arose about what to name it. Any product only becomes a brand when it is famous by name. When the question of naming the product came up, Baa suggested calling it *Pan* because that was what it was. However, Babuji disagreed. He wanted the name to be different and unique, not just a substitute for *Pan.* They felt that their product's name should stand out. Babuji sought advice from his close friends on his new startup, and one of them was Acharya Chandak. Although Chandak, who was knowledgeable in astrology, did not propose any names, he expressed his belief that Babuji's venture would achieve unprecedented success.

Babuji was a *karmayogi* who had a keen interest in religion, spirituality, and astrology. He believed in the words of Acharya Chandak and decided to introduce his *pan masala* to the world on a large scale. He asked for suggestions from various *pan* shops to find a suitable name, but none seemed to fit. Feeling slightly clueless about a catchy and perfect brand name, he turned to Baa again for help. She suggested adding the word *parag* to the name *pan* to reflect its fragrance. Babuji was thrilled with this suggestion, and the name *Pan Parag* was ultimately chosen as the brand name. In 1973, Mansukh Bhai's long-awaited dream became a reality as he officially christened his *pan masala* blend as *Pan Parag.* The perfect mixture of ingredients, carefully selected and blended to perfection, made *Pan Parag* an irresistible choice for connoisseurs of *pan masala.* This legendary brand resulted from Mansukh Bhai's tireless hard work and dedication, which allowed him to overcome complex challenges.

The final name was chosen, but pricing and quantity were still undetermined. Packaging needed improvement. As the inventor of the product, Mansukh Bhai was fond of *pan*; he decided that 250-gram and 500-gram packaging would be convenient for customers and save them from frequent visits to the *pan* shop. At that time, tin metal packaging was in fashion, so he decided to launch the new product, *Pan Parag,* in tin packaging in the market. Despite all this, he worked daily, preparing the *Pan Parag* mixture at night and supplying *pan masala* to *pan* shops during the day as needed.

Excellent planning, perfect execution…

Mansukh Bhai was a perfectionist who never compromised on quality. He wanted his new product to have the perfect taste and packaging. He approached multinational packaging companies like Metal Box India and Poysha, but unfortunately, they couldn't fulfill his high requirements. Therefore, he had to give the contract to a local company for the tin packaging of his product.

To make *Pan Parag* more unique and attractive, Babuji suggested adding a small spoon to the package. This idea helped make *Pan Parag* more popular at that time. Mansukh Bhai's excellent planning and execution helped make *Pan Parag* a successful product.

He shifted his attention to the logo and packaging design of the *Pan Parag* brand after successfully solving the packaging problem. He consulted with some local people for their opinions but still felt something needed to be added. Due to his passion for this brand, he moved to Delhi to continue his search for the missing piece. He contacted several advertising agencies and discussed with many experts there. It took him almost a week, but he persevered tirelessly to find the perfect combination. They showed him all the designs and drawings, but he still wanted more. Many suggestions were made, such as *King of Pan Masala* and *Hazaaron Ki Pasand,* but none satisfied him. Finally, his journey led him to a famous advertising agency of that time, and on 18 August 1973, he launched his revolutionary product *Pan Parag* in the market, which later became the number one brand.

Deepak Bhai also started taking its supplies when *Pan Parag* was launched in the rainy days of August. However, a new problem arose within a week. *Pan Parag* was packed in tin boxes, but moisture had become its enemy. *Pan Parag* would turn red during rainy days due to slight humidity. Deepak Bhai and his team started bringing back double the quantity of *Pan Parag* they used to supply. As with any new product, there were initial challenges, but risk management expert Mansukh Bhai skillfully addressed them. Despite the growing demand, the monsoon season brought about mounting losses. Even in these circumstances, Babuji did not accept defeat and found a solution. As long as the weather was terrible, he reduced production and supplies. Babuji knew that those who had tasted his *Pan Parag* would definitely ask for it, but due to a small supply, it would be sold even after turning red. In this way, the loss would be reduced, but due to less supply, the demand among people would remain. There was no other *pan masala* at that time, so he had no fear of any other competitor getting established in the market.

When the rainy season ended, Babuji again sped up the production of *Pan Parag*. But the demand started exceeding the supply, and he needed a bigger space and a warehouse. In this matter, he got full support from home. Some things in the house were packed up, and some space was freed up. Machinery was also required to make products. He somehow managed all this but needed help to supply the product relative to the market demand. For this, he started needing more space, money, and workers. Baa freed up even more space in the house. Everyone worked day and night on mixing and packaging, and Babuji delivered the finished product to the market. Gradually, he set up a factory by acquiring a separate place for this, where he began producing his products on a large scale.

Craze for aroma and taste...

The unique aroma and flavour of the product gradually gained popularity in nearby districts and towns. *Pan* shops started selling *Pan Parag* as a popular gift for people residing in outlying areas. Even in Kanpur, Babuji started giving *Pan Parag* as a gift to his acquaintances and relatives whenever he visited them. The product's popularity grew as whoever tasted it once became hooked to its aroma and taste. Babuji had to hire many distributors and use passenger trains to keep up with the increasing demand for the supply. Although he faced several challenges with production, packaging, promotion, advertising, and distribution, fate is said to be kind to brave people, and something similar happened to Babuji.

Mansukh Bhai now had big plans to launch *Pan Parag* nationwide and sought a unique punchline to promote the product. Although he received many suggestions from various agencies, none resonated with him. Ultimately, he found a punch-line to help *Pan Parag* stand out - *Dhoom macha de, Rang jama de.* This choice of punchline proved wise; till today, it is considered one of the top 10 punchlines. Mansukh Bhai was now completely immersed in the world of *Pan Parag* and his dream was to create a sensation across the country. He began to plan for its national launch, and in the same year, his second son, Deepak Bhai Kothari, fully joined him in the business. Together, they made *Pan Parag* a success story that grew by leaps and bounds every day. Mansukh Bhai's hard work and dedication paid off, and he achieved a success he never thought possible. His wife, Sharda Ben, was also an equal partner in this success. As Robert Collier, the American author of self-help and New Thought metaphysical books, said, "*Success is the sum of small efforts, repeated every day.*" Mansukh Bhai's extraordinary success can be defined by these words. He left his village with a dream, and with hard work and perseverance, he accomplished more than he had ever imagined.

Babuji understood the significance of developing public relations, even when it was not yet common practice. He believed that expanding one's network was crucial to achieving success. Babuji always made time for suppliers, packagers, distributors, retailers, advertising agencies, and company employees. He also believed that one should be determined to take one's product everywhere people could go. This approach played a vital role in the success of *Pan Parag*. The product dominated the market in a tin box from 1973 to 1985.

What set Babuji apart was that despite the immense success of *Pan Parag*, he continued to explore other businesses. In 1979, he took over the 'Parle Flash Dental Cream' agency. Babuji launched the cream in Kanpur and nearby markets, but the product failed to take off despite carrying the name Parle. Due to the heavy workload of *Pan Parag* every day, Babuji eventually abandoned the business of all Parle products in 1981.

After achieving financial success and gaining prestige in society, Mansukh Bhai began to worry about those who were often neglected. He felt the need to do something for his community.

As a result, Babuji established the 'Sharda Mansukh Bhai Kothari Charitable Trust' in 1980.

No work was considered small...

Mansukh Bhai was a man of great wisdom and inspiring values. His father's struggles taught him the importance of honesty and self-trust. These values propelled him to take up his first job as a supervisor of sanitation workers, earning a meagre salary of 80 paise per month. From there, he embarked on a journey of struggle, working for *Hindustan Construction Company* for a salary of Rs. 1.25 per month. Despite the low pay, Mansukh Bhai believed that no work is small or big; people consider it as such. He thought every job could be done with confidence and dedication if one applied one's mind. He encouraged people to see obstacles as challenges and to use their minds to overcome them. Mansukh Bhai believed that life gives everyone a chance, no matter their level, and that success comes to those who seize opportunities and work hard towards their goals.

11

A New Avatar of Pan Parag, the Pouch Packaging Revolution

"Innovation is the unrelenting drive to break the status quo and develop anew where few have dared to go."

— *Steven Jeffes, Marketing and Business Expert*

In 1985, *Pan Parag* achieved a remarkable milestone that left an indelible mark on the entire FMCG and packaging industry. After almost a dozen years since its launch, the brand's popularity among *pan* connoisseurs and all sections of society was soaring high. Its demand skyrocketed, making it challenging to keep up with the supply. Yet, despite imitators trying to capitalize on its success, *Pan Parag* had already established itself as the numero uno brand, deeply rooted in people's hearts. Indeed, as the adage goes, "*one success begets another success.*" It was evident that *Pan Parag* would script another chapter of golden success.

Although the term 'innovation' has gained popularity in recent times, Deepak Bhai understood its significance four decades ago. He recognized the importance of regularly reviewing our work methods to maintain our position in the business world. He still believes that the key to increasing profits is to devise new strategies that enhance our products and boost sales – essentially, to "do something new".

The story of the 'Pouch Revolution' highlights the natural conflict between the new generation's innovative thinking and its inventor's traditional mindset towards a product. However, the conclusion of this story demonstrates that when these ideas come together, the outcomes can be incredible. After working tirelessly for almost three decades, Mansukh Bhai achieved great success. For him, *Pan Parag* was a product that represented a fulfilled dream. Meanwhile, his younger son, Deepak Bhai Kothari, who had a fresh perspective, was preparing to launch the next chapter of *Pan Parag*. He represented the vision of the upcoming generation and aimed to take *Pan Parag* out of the tin box and introduce it in pouches for the convenience of consumers. Deepak Bhai's decision was both innovative and challenging to implement, but he inherited his father's determination, who never learned to give up. For Deepak Bhai, this was a significant challenge he had to overcome to take *Pan Parag* farther than his father had envisioned.

How the revolutionary idea emerged...

Let's explore the inspiring story of the emergence of this revolutionary idea. Deepak Bhai, a visionary entrepreneur, used to brainstorm with his friends on how to elevate his product *Pan Parag* to the next level. During one of these brainstorming sessions, Deepak Bhai and his master wordsmith friend, Ashok Chaturvedi, came up with a groundbreaking concept that nobody had ever thought of before. They realized that the key to disrupting the industry was to present *Pan Parag* in a fresh, new avatar - the sachet. Pouch packaging was the solution to creating an unprecedented success story for the leading brand. Deepak Bhai's innovative thinking changed the game forever, marking a new era of progress in the industry.

Deepak Bhai is a passionate reader and learner who enjoys exploring the works of famous writers and reading articles on various topics. His visionary thinking made him realize that flexible packaging, such as sealed or stand-up pouches, would be the future of packaging due to its numerous benefits and resource efficiency. Ashok Chaturvedi recognized Deepak's unwavering determination to promote pouch packaging and offered to collaborate with him on this mission without hesitation.

Selling *Pan Parag* in boxes took a lot of work. The boxes were bulky and heavy, making transportation a considerable challenge. Although the demand for *Pan Parag* was increasing, it required significant effort to supply it. *Pan* lovers also started adding *pan parag* to *pan* leaves, and *pan* vendors asked for smaller containers. Ashok Chaturvedi used to run the plastic foil and paper business, so he immediately took up the pouch idea. Interestingly, nothing like this existed in the country or abroad, yet both friends decided to start their search process locally, i.e., in Kanpur. The real challenge that Deepak Bhai faced was convincing Babuji to adopt the pouch idea.

Ashok Chaturvedi searched for a pouch in Kanpur but couldn't find any information about it. This was not surprising because pouches were not even made at that time. Deepak Bhai asked Ashok Chaturvedi a few days later if he had seen the pouch. Ashok replied that the pouch was unavailable and would have to be made. However, Kanpur's machine owners and operators were unwilling to make it. When asked why, Ashok said that no one knew how to make it, and the only option was to gather information from abroad. Ashok suggested that Japan or Taiwan could be possible places to find information. But Deepak Bhai needed permission from Babuji to travel abroad.

Babuji's principles and Deepak Bhai's insistence...

Babuji was a person of strong principles when it came to business matters. On the other hand, Deepak Bhai was hesitant to discuss the matter with him. He had many questions, such as whether to tell Babuji what to say if he did and whether Babuji would approve any changes. Babuji was strictly against changes in *Pan Parag*, which was a matter of prestige for him

Deepak Bhai has inherited all the qualities of his father, Babuji. After much contemplation, he decided to share his innovative idea with Babuji. He believed that if Babuji refused, he would tell his mother Baa. Since Babuji valued Baa's words, Deepak Bhai hoped he would listen to her. One evening during dinner, when the entire family gathered, Deepak Bhai tried to express his views to Babuji. However, he could not speak as other family members, or Babuji himself started talking. As a result, he waited until nightfall and went to Babuji's room, where Baa was also present. When he entered the room, Babuji looked at his son curiously. Feeling nervous and confused, Deepak Bhai began to speak.

Deepak Bhai's voice trembled as he spoke to Mansukh Bhai, "*Bauji,* I want to start a new innings of *Pan Parag* and I need your blessings...". Mansukh Bhai did not reply but his eyes remained fixed on his son's face.

Deepak Bhai continued, saying, "Babuji, I have an idea to package *Pan Parag* in a pouch as well...."

Mansukh Bhai was not pleased with this idea and responded, "No, this cannot be possible. You know what *Pan Parag* represents and it has a special identity...."

Deepak Bhai tried to persuade him and said, "Babuji, just think about it... If *Pan Parag* comes in a pouch, it will be within everyone's reach... Its sales will increase and so will the business...."

Despite Deepak Bhai's argument, Mansukh Bhai refused to accept his proposal and asked him to leave the spot.

Deepak Bhai had made a decision and expected praise, encouragement, and a pat on the back from Babuji. However, Babuji strongly protested against the decision. Babuji believed that *Pan Parag* was a tradition that held a different status and respect in society. The tin box on which *Pan Parag* was displayed was also a part of its identity, and Babuji was sensitive about the brand's reputation in the market. Although Deepak Bhai explained the advantages of the pouch to Babuji, including its ability to reach more customers, Babuji remained opposed to the idea. Baa was also present but did not take sides. Baa knew Mansukh Bhai would never agree to something he did not like.

After some time, Baa came out of the room, and Deepak Bhai requested that she convince Babuji to let him start *Pan Parag* in the pouch. Deepak Bhai also revealed his plan to travel abroad to his mother. She wanted to see her son progress but didn't want to make her husband sad. After some time, she said to Deepak, "Wait, I will talk to him. Maybe he will agree."

Baa again entered Babuji's room and talked to him before Deepak Bhai. Baa said, "Look, Deepak's pouch idea looks good. He is working very hard on it. Like you, he also wants to take the business to new heights. Please agree for the pouch. If you don't encourage your sons, then who will?" Baa made many more emotional statements as if she was trying to persuade her husband in this way. Mansukh Bhai loved his wife very much. At last, he reluctantly agreed to the pouch idea on his wife's insistence.

Mansukh Bhai, "Okay…if you say so, then it is okay…but see…the glory of *Pan Parag* should not be diminished…." After many requests, Mansukh Bhai permitted Deepak Bhai to explore the pouch idea abroad. Babuji once said later that he felt that even going abroad would not do anything about the pouch, and there was no harm in allowing Deepak to try.

Searched extensively first in Japan, then in Taiwan

Deepak Bhai traveled to Japan with permission from Babuji. He carried 15 bulky samples of *Pan Parag* in his bags and even hired a translator. However, upon arriving in Japan, he realized there was an issue with the pouch packaging of the product there. Things did not work out as he expected. He then moved to Taiwan, where he faced the challenge of finding pouch packaging for the product. He searched extensively but could not find a pouch and was still looking for packaging or similar products. He then contacted several large machine companies in Taiwan but was still looking for a solution. Throughout his week-long stay in Taiwan, Deepak Bhai spent his days exploring the markets with *Pan Parag,* looking for solutions, but he returned to his hotel each evening without any results. He faced many difficulties, including travelling all day and not finding any suitable food options. Despite extensive travels to China, Japan, Taiwan, and Hong Kong, his quest for the dream pouch continued to elude him, but he remained determined.

The search was becoming endless; at this point, Deepak Bhai again thought out of the box and decided to have the pouch blocks made locally in Taiwan using lathe machines instead of a company. With the help of an interpreter, he discussed the idea with several local Taiwanese retail artisans. After much effort, a Taiwanese engineer agreed to build the block. He made a block, filled it with *Pan Parag,* and then showed it to Deepak Bhai. However, Deepak Bhai was concerned about the quantity, i.e., how big the pouch should be and how much *masala* it should contain. He returned to the hotel, and it was clear that the pouch had been made and the *masala* had also been filled in, but the problem had arisen regarding the quantity. Just a day before coming to India, Deepak Bhai decided that the pouch could be 100 grams, 500 grams, and 10 grams. His close friend Ashok was with him during this time, so he helped Deepak Bhai and suggested making 100 and 10-gram blocks. They asked the lathe machine owner to make the blocks and fill them with *pan masala*. When the lathe owner showed the pouch he had made, Ashok and Deepak Bhai were delighted. However, the matter was still complicated as they needed to figure out how the blocks would be transported to India and assembled. Additionally, they needed to find a way to produce more such blocks.

Had a narrow escape in an earthquake in Japan

Deepak Bhai faced many challenges in realizing his dream of the 'Pouch Revolution'. However, nothing could have prepared him for the devastating earthquake that struck the same city in Japan while he was there. The quake was much stronger than average. Fortunately, he narrowly escaped the disaster by God's grace. Despite the earthquake, Japan's exceptional disaster management system ensured that he was safely evacuated. The earthquake made things even more challenging for Deepak Bhai, as he struggled to find his favourite food and faced communication barriers despite having an interpreter.

Deepak Bhai thought inviting the engineer to India would be more beneficial. He would create the block, transport it, and assemble it upon arrival. Once the engineer presented it, the artisans in Kanpur would take over and complete the work.

Deepak Bhai shared the problem with the Taiwanese engineer and sought help from him. He offered to cover all expenses if the engineer could come to India and create a pouch. The engineer agreed to travel to India to assist. Upon arrival, Deepak Bhai discussed the progress of the pouch project with Babuji, but he was not enthusiastic. Deepak Bhai realized that the path to achieving success was still tricky. Therefore, he invited the Taiwanese engineer to India without informing Mansukh Bhai. Using the assistance of local lathe workers in Kanpur, they began experimenting with making sachets for *Pan Parag.* After a few days of trial and error, they developed a 10-gram sachet. They printed the name on the pouch and matched the colour to that of the *Pan Parag* boxes. When the pouch was completed, Deepak Bhai was thrilled with the outcome.

Fantastic work of Taiwanese engineer...

The Taiwanese engineer made remarkable contributions in Kanpur by creating pouches of varying shapes and sizes, designing them beautifully, and selecting their colours. He also trained several lathe workers in Kanpur. After obtaining Babuji's approval, a blockchain was developed, and *Pan Parag* began to be manufactured in sachets. Preparations were made for its official launch, marking a breakthrough in the packaging industry that began in Kanpur, with Deepak Bhai as its pioneer.

The idea became the foundation of the world's first pouch packaging!

In the 1980s, edible items in pouches were a unique and innovative idea. Deepak Bhai envisioned that small packaging would be the future, enabling maximum reach to customers and easy storage, making the products affordable for everyone. He had shared his determination with his family and colleagues, and on his birthday, 26 June 1985, *Pan Parag* was launched in pouch packaging, marking the beginning of a successful revolution. Deepak Bhai's vision paved the way for small enterprises to expand and create new employment opportunities, thus promoting industrial growth in the country. Although the launch of sachets gave rise to several competitors, Deepak Bhai's step proved highly beneficial for *Pan Parag* and other products. His innovative idea became the foundation of the world's first pouch packaging, and the *Pan Parag* sachet packaging was also launched with great enthusiasm in Japan-Taiwan.

And the pouch was an instant hit...

Pan Parag was launched in the pouch, but Deepak Bhai feared that if it did not work in the market, then Babuji might issue orders to close it. Due to this, it would take him only a short time to lose his reputation and credibility in Babuji's eyes. To avoid having to listen to Babuji's scolding and face him, Deepak Bhai travelled abroad with his wife, Aarti Kothari. Then, one day, a telegram came from Babuji in which he wrote, "Deepak, miracle has happened... your pouch has become a great hit." In this way, Mansukh Bhai had written down everything he had in his heart.

Deepak Bhai jumped with joy after hearing about the success of the pouch. Soon after this, Deepak Bhai returned to Kanpur. On the other hand, the success of the *Pan Parag* sachet gave great satisfaction to Babuji and also strengthened his belief that his son Deepak Bhai would not only be able to handle his legacy and business well but would also take it beyond his imagination. Even after the launch of the pouch, Babuji never allowed any compromise with quality at any cost. He kept the products at par with international standards. He used to observe every activity very attentively and was interested in knowing people's opinions. He knew well how to 'connect' his brand with the public.

For this reason, he used to associate words related to people with his brand. This was seen in their brands, like Seven Up Coconut Oil, *Pan Parag,* Budget Detergent, Yes mineral water, and many other products. He trusted his employees and had complete faith in working with team spirit. This was why there was no looking back once *Pan Parag* started quickly climbing the ladder of success in tins and sachets. *Pan Parag* created such a stir in the market that its influence has persisted till date.

12

A Great Out-of-the-Box Thinker

"Big ideas come from forward thinking people who challenge the norm, think outside the box, and invent the world they see inside rather than submitting to the limitations of current dilemmas."

— Thomas Dexter Jakes, American Motivational Speaker

Mansukh Bhai was an exceptional individual who stood out like pure gold amidst the turbulence of life. He believed that to succeed and become a shining example for others, one must approach everything with great enthusiasm and a unique style. Whether celebrating, learning the intricacies of business, entering the market, launching a product, or creating an advertisement, Mansukh Bhai did it all with flair and passion. He was living proof that success comes to those who do everything joyfully and passionately.

The story behind the iconic ad...

When Mansukh Bhai envisioned taking his innovative product to the national level, he believed that a powerful and captivating advertisement was the key to communicating the essence of *Pan Parag's* fragrance to the entire nation. Mansukh Bhai wanted to create an ad that would appeal to *pan* enthusiasts and ordinary people alike and inspire them to relish the taste of *Pan Parag*. He aimed to introduce this delicious treat to everyone, even those unfamiliar with the *pan* world. To achieve his goal, he travelled to Mumbai, Surat, Ahmedabad, and Delhi to seek the advice of some of the biggest names in advertising. With a clear vision, he explained precisely what he needed for the ad to make *Pan Parag* a household name.

He clearly stated that the advertisement should not be copied or similar to any other company's product. Experts in the advertising industry presented many scripts to Mansukh Bhai, but he found them below his expectations. One admirable quality of Mansukh Bhai was that he was not influenced by even the most famous and influential people. He would only accept work once he was satisfied. Mansukh Bhai would immediately reject the ideas of those who had created advertisements for big companies. He used to say, "If I don't understand it, how will the audience like it?" He believed that ads should be pleasing to the eye, be connected to society, and make people feel like they belong. The product sales may remain the same after the advertisement, but people from every corner of the country should be aware of the product.

After several meetings, Mansukh Bhai approved a script presented by a renowned advertising agency. However, he provided many suggestions for revisions. While the story was based on his suggestions, he later expressed dissatisfaction with it, prompting the creation of a new script. After another ten to twelve meetings, the new script was finalized. Then, the question of who would act in the advertisement film arose. Babuji suggested great actors Shammi Kapoor and Ashok Kumar for the project. However, the advertising agency refused, citing their high fees and lack of interest in promoting a new product. Despite this, Mansukh Bhai was determined to see his vision come to life and urged the agency to convince the actors to participate. He emphasized that money was not the issue as long as the work was innovative and outstanding.

Babuji cast a spell on legendary actors!

Two veteran Bollywood stars, Shammi Kapoor and Ashok Kumar, had never acted together in their careers. Babuji wanted to bring them together in an advertising film, which was a big deal then. When the advertising agency approached Shammi Kapoor and Ashok Kumar, the great actors hesitated to do the advertisement and avoided the matter. When this information was given to Mansukh Bhai, he was not disappointed. He decided to meet both the actors, but meeting actors in *Mayanagari* takes more work. Somehow, Babuji was introduced to both the actors. It was as if Babuji had cast a spell on them during the meeting. He impressed Shammi Kapoor and Ashok Kumar with his story so much that both the actors happily agreed to act in his advertisement. When this advertisement was ready, even its creators had no idea of its impact.

75th birthday and the magic of Ashaji's voice...

In the year 2000, Babuji celebrated his 75th birthday in grand style. Despite his busy business schedule, Babuji always found a way to balance his life and live it to the fullest. To make the occasion truly special, he invited the legendary Bollywood playback singer Asha Bhosle to perform. And what a performance it was! Asha Bhosle's enchanting voice mesmerized the guests and made Babuji's birthday unforgettable. Even today, people still talk about that magical celebration.

Remarkable patience and the story of Kuber...

Once, there was an incident where Babuji kept some money in his company's safe. He used to keep money in the safe after daily calculations, and only his son, Deepak Bhai, and a trusted employee, Kuber, were aware of it. The rest of the people in the company were not aware of this. The next day, Babuji needed money for some work and took the money from the safe. Babuji habitually counted cash while keeping it in the safe and taking it out. When Babuji counted the money after taking it out from the safe, there was one note less in it. Babuji counted the money again and found less money, so he got worried. Babuji knew that apart from him, sometimes Kuber opened that safe, and sometimes Deepak Bhai opened it. So, he called Kuber to discuss the issue. It was no small matter for money to go missing from the safe.

After Kuber was summoned to his chamber, Mansukh Bhai said calmly, "Kuber, did anyone open the safe after me?"

Kuber replied, "No, Babuji, I don't know."

Mansukh Bhai said, "You take money from the safe and give it to me... that's why I asked. One note is missing from the money that was kept."

Kuber felt worried. "Babuji, I don't know about this," he said, becoming silent. Strange thoughts started coming to Kuber's mind, and he became terrified. Mansukh Bhai looked at Kuber carefully and said, "Don't worry... tell me if you remember... okay... go..."

After hearing this, Kuber left the spot. Instead of doubting Kuber, Mansukh Bhai wondered who could take a note. Where would this note have gone? Had it been someone else, he might have swiftly taken action and dismissed the employee, but Mansukh Bhai had a great deal of trust in Kuber. Kuber had lived up to his trust many times. That's why Mansukh Bhai did not doubt him but kept wondering where the note had gone. He remembered that Deepak Bhai also kept money in the safe, so maybe he had withdrawn the money. Mansukh Bhai immediately called his son Deepak Bhai.

Mansukh Bhai asked flatly, "Deepak... did you take out money from the safe?"

Deepak Bhai: "Babuji, I did not take it out... The safe remains locked. You also have the key..."

On hearing this, Mansukh Bhai simply said to his son, "Okay."

Mansukh Bhai was extremely upset, but he did not lose patience. He kept wondering where the Rs. 500 note had gone... He opened the safe again and counted all the money... but the Rs. 500 note still needed to be found. The whole day passed in this confusion. Suddenly, an idea struck his mind in the evening. When he put his hand under the top drawer of the safe, he found a Rs. 500 note stuck in it. After retrieving the note, Babuji felt satisfied; but he had deep trust in Kuber and Deepak Bhai. This incident shows that Mansukh Bhai may have done everything in a measured manner, but honesty and trust were his actual wealth. In this respect, he had immense trust in his people. If he wanted, he could have talked to all the employees. He could have interrogated everyone. He could have scolded everyone by losing his temper, but patience was Mansuk Bhai's biggest asset since childhood. Because of that patience, he was confident that the money would not have gone anywhere. Babuji used to say, "*Every employee, officer, distributor, and every person associated with Kothari Products and every person who consumes the goods of Kothari Products is a part of the Kothari family. He has full faith in people's engagement and the loyalty of his employees.*"

He made crucial and vital decisions only after listening to his inner voice, based on this 'trust.' He possessed truly extraordinary, out-of-the-box thinking.

Diwali celebration left people mesmerized!

The launch of *Pan Parag* in the market was followed by a fantastic event that left an unforgettable impression on the people of Kanpur. Babuji decided to celebrate Diwali like never before, inviting all *Pan Parag* employees, their families, and children to the office for a grand celebration. The joy of the attendees was overwhelming as they received gifts such as clothes, toys, sweets, and fireworks. The city was left mesmerized as they witnessed the grandeur of Babuji's Diwali celebration. Countless lights were lit in front of his office on Mall Road, and by nightfall, the sky was filled with beautiful fireworks. Firecrackers echoed throughout the entire Civil Lines area, leaving an indelible mark on the people's minds. Babuji's Diwali celebration was genuinely worth seeing.

MMK

13

MMK Stands for Money, Marketing and Knowledge

"Real talent shines through regardless of how many others there are around you."

— Paloma Faith, British Singer

Mansukh Bhai Mahadev Bhai Kothari, also known as MMK, was an extraordinary individual who lived up to his name. Though he appeared to be just an ordinary person, he possessed an incredible talent and personality that set him apart from others. His colleagues and friends often joked that the acronym 'MMK' was the complete form of his name, as he genuinely embodied the qualities associated with those letters.

M = Money

M = Marketing

K = Knowledge

According to Babuji, three things are necessary for achieving success and earning a profit in business: 'M' for money, 'M' for marketing, and 'K' for knowledge. Despite having less formal education, Mansukh Bhai inherited business skills from his father and continued to enhance them. He supervised cleaning work, counted bricks, ran the canteen, hawked, brought goods from Calcutta, and sold them in Lucknow and Kanpur. He derived his marketing tips from hands-on experience rather than theoretical books. By learning natural marketing tricks and continuously improving them, he acquired the necessary skills to succeed in business.

Mansukh Bhai's five business principles...

Mansukh Bhai followed five business principles. During the early struggle, he purchased goods from Calcutta and sold them in the Lucknow-Kanpur region. This was challenging because people needed more money, and fashion was not prevalent then. Despite these challenges, he brought expensive cigarettes, cosmetics, and other daily-use items and travelled in the general class on trains to save money. He even convinced the train ticket examiner to transport his goods to Kanpur—however, his real struggle would begin after this point.

Mansukh Bhai believed that more than merely having a good variety of items was required; the real challenge was to find buyers for the goods, convince them that what he was selling was unique and of high quality, and ensure that the goods were affordable and one-of-a-kind. This was a daunting task, and modern-day marketers must spend a lot of money to create a market for something new. They must advertise, offer goods on credit, make stockists and dealers, and, most importantly, generate demand. However, Mansukh Bhai managed to market his products brilliantly, even when people tried to minimize their expenses. He carefully marketed goods that were not considered urgent needs; without them, people's lives would not have been impacted.

Mansukh Bhai had an extraordinary talent for persuading people to spend money, even during a time when saving money was seen as a sign of success. His marketing skills were exceptional, and he had a remarkable ability to sell everything he sourced, leaving nothing unsold. Mansukh Bhai, while discussing the five main points of the business with his colleagues, often used to say that *any product can be successful in the market only if it is beautiful. Secondly, if it is of high quality; thirdly, if it is incomparable to similar products. It may not be cheaper than the others, but it should be in the same range, fourthly, it should be available everywhere in the market, and fifthly, people should have correct information about it.* He made a lot of money in all kinds of businesses. In the present era, people become satisfied after earning a little money. When the business is running well, we become engrossed in it. After establishing the company, people hesitate to enter a new one. Despite lacking capital sometimes, Mansukh Bhai continued to venture into new businesses because of his expertise and honesty.

Had an unyielding thirst for knowledge

He was a great listener and enjoyed participating in discussions about the country, the world, business, and society. Even when he took time off from business, he would converse with his friends and carefully listen to their ideas, retaining anything valuable. This unyielding thirst for knowledge set him apart from others his age, making him an astute businessman. When he worked at the canteen in Avadi, Karnataka, he would ride his bicycle to the market to buy vegetables and negotiate their prices to understand the difference between wholesale and retail prices. This habit continued when he brought goods from Calcutta to Kanpur, where he would bargain for goods instead of buying everything from one place. Mansukh Bhai's dedication to gaining knowledge and exceptional business acumen helped him expand his business and capital and earn the respect of society.

He was an excellent business connoisseur...

Mansukh Bhai's exceptional expertise in business took *Pan Parag* to great heights, becoming an example for the whole world to follow. He was not a magician but an outstanding business connoisseur and a tremendously hard worker. His commitment to keeping his businesses at the forefront of the market made him a true leader. His formula of money-marketing knowledge was the key to his success. He invested, earned, and made more money, and his brilliant use of resources is still an example to emulate. His dedication and passion for his work made him honest and reliable, and his success inspired many. His money-marketing-knowledge formula will continue to guide people toward success, and his legacy of excellence will forever be remembered.

He could visualize the next ten years!

There is a quote by the famous author Malcolm Gladwell: "A visionary leader starts with a clean sheet of paper and reimagines the world." Despite not being an avid reader, Mansukh Bhai was gifted with a crystal-clear vision. He could see the picture of the next ten years and adapt his business accordingly. In the nineties, he ventured into other business sectors, keeping pace with the changing times. He launched an ambitious investment plan in the real estate sector. The group has a strong presence in metropolitan cities such as Bengaluru, Hyderabad, Kochi, Kolkata, Mumbai, and Pune. Presently, the group owns commercial buildings in Bengaluru, Mumbai, and Pune, which are leased to top multinational IT companies. Moreover, the group is developing several hotels and serviced apartments in Kolkata and Lavasa. The Group is a powerhouse in international trading, dealing in a diverse range of commodities such as coal, electric and electronic items, construction materials, chemicals, and agro-based products. Its shares are traded on both the Bombay Stock Exchange and the National Stock Exchange, with a long-standing history of consecutive dividend declarations - a testament to its unwavering commitment to creating wealth for its stakeholders. This is all thanks to the visionary leadership of Babuji.

PAN PARAG

14

Father of the Pan Masala Industry

"Exceptional leaders go beyond the norm to enhance
the confidence of their groups and staff.
Once people start trusting themselves,
there is no limit to what they can achieve."

— *Anonymous.*

Mansukh Bhai was considered a pioneer in the *pan masala* industry. His dedication, intelligence, courage, and leadership skills earned him the title of 'Father of the *pan masala* industry'. He invented *pan masala* and played a crucial role in establishing and branding the industry with his *Pan Parag* brand. He secured the industry's corporate status through his remarkable efforts, ensuring its future.

A trendsetter in the advertising world...

Mansukh Bhai was also a trailblazer in advertising when the industry was not yet well-established in the country. He introduced a series of widespread and large-scale advertisements featuring well-known personalities to promote the distinct features of his various products. Even before it gained widespread popularity, he recognized the significance of advertising through the television industry. Mansukh Bhai became well-known for promoting his *Pan Parag* commercials on popular TV shows. More than forty-five years ago, he recognized the power, reach, and influence of television and was the first to introduce Fast-Moving Consumer Goods (FMCG) to the small screen.

The magic of advertisements continues to captivate

Mansukh Bhai firmly believed in excellence and never compromised on quality, no matter the cost. Despite his busy schedule, he closely monitored everything from copywriting to designing advertisements. This attention to detail ensured that every line of the ads he chose remained on people's lips long after they aired. Unsurprisingly, the fantastic magic of every line of the script of the advertisements he chose is still on people's lips. He had learned the importance of this approach through his experiences in launching and marketing various products. Mansukh Bhai preferred to do everything himself and always took the lead in every aspect of his work. *Sathe Biscuits, Jyoti Brahmi Amla Oil, Seven Up Coconut Oil, OK Soap, Parle G Biscuit, Chhotabhai Beedi, Budget Detergent Powder, Yes Namkeen, Yes Mineral Water,* and his dream product *Pan Parag* were enough to give him the status of a patriarch in the industry. His packaging was always excellent, and he strongly believed that any product should reach the public beautifully with its quality; even if it takes time, it should have perfection.

No less than an advertising guru

It wouldn't be an exaggeration to say that Mansukh Bhai was nothing less than an advertising guru. He had a knack for getting celebrities like Jalal Aga, Vijayendra Ghatge, Hema Malini, Sarika, Ayesha Jhulka, Saeed Jaffrey, Ashok Kumar, Shammi Kapoor, Alok

Nath, Reema Lagoo, Ronit Roy and Sachin Kelkar to endorse his products. He was open to experimenting with different advertising genres and was never afraid to take risks. He also sponsored cricket tournaments and promoted films. Mansukh Bhai was aware of the importance of print media and advertised his products in magazines like *Stardust* and *Filmfare*. He was an expert in outdoor advertising and personally assessed prime locations for his ads. He would ride his motorcycle to these locations and conduct surveys to determine the perfect size and form of the advertisements to ensure maximum visibility.

He also celebrated the country's glorious moments, like the cricket match between India and Pakistan. A glimpse of such things can also be seen in the advertisements for his products. His advertisement on the front page of *India Today*'s popular Hindi magazine was exceptional and is still considered a prime example of effective advertising. He even actively engaged with people to celebrate the launch of 'Samjhauta Express' in the country through an animated TV programme. His unique punchlines in his advertisements are widely recognized, and these punchlines generated a lot of buzz, and people still remember and hum them even today:

* *The Choice of Millions*
* *Dhoom Macha De, Rang Jama De*
* *Ek Se Mera Kya Hoga*
* *Baratiyon Ka Swagat Pan Parag Se Kijiye*
* *Pyara Sa Swad, Bandhe Sabko Sath*
* *The Choice of Young India*
* *Pan Parag Khaya Kya*

Thanks to his unique qualities, Babuji pioneered the Pan Masala industry. He established his own identity as a successful businessman and had a deep understanding of the world, from packaging to advertising. Babuji introduced new directions for food products and made advertisers aware of their features, emphasizing the importance of promoting them. He was decades ahead in sponsoring sports events and used his product *Pan Parag* to promote sports. In recognition of his contributions, Babuji was honoured with the *National Citizen Award* by Prime Minister Rajiv Gandhi on 2 August 1989. He was also awarded the *Gaurav Ratna Award* at the Bangkok Conference of Non-Resident Indians in 1992 and the *Zee Cine Award* in 2004. Babuji received many other honours both in India and abroad.

Pan Parag continues to make waves worldwide, following Mansukh Bhai's tradition of providing the best products to consumers. Last year, the Golden Jubilee of *Pan Parag* was celebrated to honour Mansukh Bhai's remarkable legacy, visionary leadership, and marketing wizardness. His contributions as a first-generation entrepreneur who achieved patriarch status in the *pan masala* industry were commemorated with great admiration and respect. His legacy is one that will never be forgotten.

The miracle of advertising strategy!

Mansukh Bhai was a visionary who understood the importance of social responsibility in business. He utilized his product advertisements to raise social awareness—one such ad *Baratiyon Ka Swagat Pan Parag Se Kijiye* (Welcome the wedding procession with *Pan Parag*) was an excellent example of his anti-dowry campaign that left a lasting impression on people. Mansukh Bhai's unique advertising strategy worked wonders as he transformed *Pan Parag* into a social product. It became a symbol of social harmony and a custom to serve at gatherings and weddings, breaking all caste, religion, and wealth barriers. The impact of his approach was truly awe-inspiring.

SECTION 3

Humility is the true key to success. Successful people lose their way at times. They often embrace and overindulge in the fruits of success. Humility halts this arrogance and self-indulging trap. Humble people share the credit and wealth, remaining focused and hungry to continue the journey of success.

— Rick Pitino, American Basketball Coach

15

Nothing Is Impossible

There is only one thing that makes a dream impossible to achieve. And that is the fear of failure.

— Paulo Coelho, Brazilian Novelist

Napoleon Bonaparte's quote, "Impossible is not in my dictionary", is well-known, but not everyone needs to have heard of it to believe in the power of determination. Mansukh Bhai was such a person - he firmly believed that anything is possible with true dedication, honesty, and a strong work ethic. He repeatedly proved his belief through his successful ventures like *Seven Up* coconut oil, *Pan Parag,* and washing powder, leaving many in awe of his ability to turn his ideas into reality. His accomplishments may remain a mystery, but the lesson he imparted is clear - with the right attitude, nothing can stop you.

In a 2022 interview, Ratan Tata, Chairman Emeritus of Tata Sons, shared that he enjoys doing work that others are unwilling to do. However, Mansukh Bhai had already embraced this philosophy 44 years before the interview. For Mansukh Bhai, the lessons he learned from life's struggles were real, and he loved taking on new challenges. Instead of being defeated by problems, he saw them as opportunities to demonstrate his abilities.

The success story of 'Budget'...

Mansukh Bhai heard about a famous washing powder in the market and decided to create a similar product. He believed that if a product from Gujarat could be successful in Kanpur and the entire state, his product could also succeed. With cheap labour available in Kanpur and no shortage of goods, Mansukh Bhai discussed his idea with Baa. Although Baa knew he would go ahead with his plans, she happily agreed to the idea of producing washing powder. This fuelled Mansukh Bhai's enthusiasm, and he quickly checked his capital accounts before conducting necessary research and understanding market demand. He also spoke with traders in the market and realized that although it was challenging to beat the washing powder of Gujarat, it was not impossible.

Mansukh Bhai was a determined man who never gave up on his ideas. He decided to launch an affordable washing powder in the market as he realized that the washing powder of the famous brand was too expensive for low-income people. While some people bought it, many preferred locally available discounted soap as it was more affordable. Even some established businessmen could not sell Gujarat's washing powder in the market as they desired. After discussing this issue with his close friends and thinking about it for a few days, Mansukh Bhai decided on the name for his brand - *Budget*. This brand name perfectly reflected his commitment to breaking the cycle of unaffordability and providing affordable washing powder to those who needed it most.

When he again shared the story with his supportive and encouraging wife, she agreed to name the product *Budget*. On 18 August 1988, *Budget Washing Powder* was launched with a grand ceremony in Kanpur. A great advertisement was also created to promote Budget Washing Powder. The marketing strategy was to popularize Budget Washing Powder by emphasizing its ability to provide more washing at a lower price. It was a unique selling point compared to the competitor's washing powder, which only came in one-kilo packs.

Mansukh Bhai introduced half-kilo and 200-gram packs of his budget washing powder alongside the original one-kilo pack to make it more accessible to consumers. This strategy proved to be successful, as the budget washing powder became immensely popular in a short amount of time. It provided tough competition to the already-established washing powder brand and solidified its place. This success story is a testament to Mansukh Bhai's determination and willingness to tackle any challenge. Even after the success of his previous venture, *Pan Parag*, he remained hungry for new business opportunities and always sought to take his ventures to new heights. The word 'impossible' had no place in his life; he relished facing challenges and constantly sought new ones.

Recognized the power of collaboration 44 years ago!

Forty-four years ago, the visionary Babuji recognized the immense power of collaboration in achieving success. He astutely established a comprehensive organization to conduct business and formed strategic partnerships with other establishments. Babuji firmly believed that although he had already achieved significant success, the future necessitated us to work together in solidarity and support each other. By fostering a culture of collaboration and mutual support, Babuji achieved his goals and paved the way for future generations to follow in his footsteps and achieve greatness through collective effort.

16

Down to Earth, Even While Touching the Skies

A tree is known by its fruit; a man by his deeds. A good deed is never lost; he who sows courtesy reaps friendship, and he who plants kindness gathers love.

– St Basil the Great

The exhilaration of achieving extraordinary success can sometimes gradually affect a person's mental equilibrium to such an extent that he/she might not even realize when qualities like humility and purity of heart disappear from the personality. It is a bitter truth that most highly successful people tend to forget their roots and deliberately keep a distance from their loved ones, but Mansukh Bhai was different. He believed – *The airplane may fly in the sky, but it can only take off and land on the ground.So keep learning with a blackbox mindset and stay humble.*

Mansukh Bhai's statement reveals two qualities that made him truly inspirational. Firstly, he had an insatiable thirst for knowledge, eager to learn something new every day and every moment. Secondly, he was driven by his desire to see his own people and everyone around him happy. When he travelled from Narali village to Kanpur, he envisioned a brighter future for his family, and he made it a reality by using his senses to understand Kanpur and learn the tricks of earning a profit even from the peanut seller. Throughout his life, he continued to learn and adapt, always finding new ways to earn money, fame, and wealth. However, he never let success get to his head and remained humble and grounded. Instead, he valued his relationships with others and kept them strong, always inspiring those around him.

Ensured the well-being of his loved ones

Babuji was a caring person who always looked after his loved ones. He was particularly generous towards his friends, family members, and close relatives, which was evident from how he initially gave *Pan Parag*'s agencies only to his acquaintances and relatives. It was clear that Babuji wanted to see his relatives prosper alongside him, and he tried to help them as much as he could. He always remembered his friends, many of whom were small shopkeepers, government servants, or people doing menial jobs. Despite his success and wealth, Babuji remained grounded and connected to the land. He built a luxurious office on Mall Road in Kanpur, but he still went out and met people, even when he could have just given orders to office servants. He also started travelling abroad to promote his brand and expanded his office and factory as the business grew, but he always kept in touch with people.

Simplicity was like his trademark!

Mansukh Bhai received the *President's National Award* in 1987 from the Government of India for his hard work, vision, and innovative ideas regarding investments and new startups. Giani Zail Singh, the then-President, presented him with this prestigious award. Despite receiving such a great honour, Mansukh Bhai remained humble and down-to-earth. Even after achieving tremendous success in his business, he always remembered his roots. He often visited a local sweet shop and stood by the roadside like an ordinary man, enjoying his favorite *jalebi* and *golgappa* while chatting with his friends. *Mansukh Bhai always kept in mind that his genuine well-wishers were the environment, the land, and the people who supported him during his difficult journey.* The lesson to learn from Mansukh Bhai's story is that we should never give up on simplicity.

Treated all equally regardless of financial status

Babuji's commitment to maintaining family relationships was truly remarkable. Despite his relatives' disappointing behaviour, he chose to distance himself from them dignifiedly without holding any resentment. In fact, as he became more successful, he went above and beyond to help his relatives expand their businesses, not by giving them financial aid, but by other means. Babuji firmly believed—*relationships are like capital that can be redeemed amid challenging times. Relationships are the cornerstone of our lives. They bring us joy in times of happiness and come together in times of sorrow to ease the pain.* He lived by this belief until his last breath. Throughout his life, he also remained committed to 'neither borrowing nor lending'. One of Babuji's distinctive traits was his fondness for *tea sessions.* He would engage in teaching and learning sessions while savouring a cup of tea, using it as a strategy to prolong meetings and exchange ideas. Whether it was a meeting or any other matter, Babuji always asked for only half a cup of tea. After the meeting, he would order a half cup of tea and sit longer, listening to the thoughts of the people, employees, and family members.

Mansukh Bhai was known for inspiring everyone around him. He treated all his friends respectfully, regardless of their financial status, but he never gave them crutches. Instead, he motivated them to work hard, be helpful, and do good deeds. Babuji used to advise his friends to help others only to the extent that they could survive on their own. He always emphasized the importance of being self-reliant and not becoming dependent on others. Mansukh Bhai remembered all the lessons that life had taught him, and after achieving success, he focused on the field of education, which was once a distant dream for him during his childhood.

Cared deeply for his village

Babuji's success did not change who he was. He remained committed to his roots and cared deeply for his village and childhood friends. He built a temple and a *dharamshala* and cultivated meaningful relationships. His talent for winning hearts made *Pan Parag* a tradition. Whenever his childhood friends visited him, he would welcome them with open arms. According to Mansukh Bhai, love grows stronger when we stay connected to our loved ones, family, and village. Babuji found great pleasure in fulfilling the needs of his people, and this was his most outstanding achievement. He used to say, *"Let us always remember the importance of staying connected with our village and loved ones, for it is in these relationships that we find true happiness and fulfillment."*

Baa was more than just a life partner

Baa was more than just a life partner to Mansukh Bhai - she was his equal and close friend. Every morning, before he left for work, Baa would prepare food for the day in a way that left no room for confusion. Whenever there was a problem, Baa would take charge, and Mansukh Bhai was always there to support her. They deeply understood each other's struggles and needs, which made their partnership solid and enduring. Despite financial difficulties, Mansukh Bhai continued working long hours and supporting his family. He also began spending more time at home, and while his standard of living was not luxurious, he never allowed any shortage of necessary items. As their children grew up, Baa took on the responsibility of raising them and imparting values, with Mansukh Bhai supporting her every step. Together, they created a loving and supportive family environment that stood the test of time.

17

Admired by Friends – The Life of Social Gatherings

"Friendship is the hardest thing in the world to explain. It's not something you learn in school, but if you haven't learned the meaning of friendship, you haven't learned anything."

– Muhammad Ali, American Professional Boxer

When Mansukh Bhai used to sit with his group of friends, his friends felt tremendously attracted to him. Be it financial problems or health issues, social issues, or festive occasions, despite being busy with business, he never shied away from taking time out for his friends and having fun. Once he made a friend, he remained with him for the rest of his life. Whenever the time came to test their friendship, they always stood the test. During times of struggle, Mansukh Bhai always supported his friends, and his friends too gave him all their love.

Mansukh Bhai had a reputation for being extraordinarily sociable and fun-loving. Whenever he returned home from a business trip or arrived back in Kanpur after being away, he would make it a point to meet up with his friends. He enjoyed spending time with them on street corners or in nooks, engaging in lively conversations and joking. His remarkable charm and sweetness endeared him to all who knew him. He was always willing to listen to his friends' problems and offer his help and advice. He was known to have a sharp mind and a knack for finding solutions to any issue. He remained optimistic and positive even in difficult times, never allowing his struggles to dampen the mood. His friends respected him for his unwavering positivity and ability to quickly handle any situation.

In times of success, Mansukh Bhai's friends would gather regularly to celebrate. They would all meet at the Mall Road office in the evenings, indulging in delicious chaat-pakodas while engaging in light-hearted gossip. Along with their everyday conversations, they also discussed business and exchanged valuable insights. The group would order mouth-watering chaat, jalebi, and kachori from Birhana Road to add to their joyful gatherings. Mansukh Bhai was always focused on his work and never allowed people to sit idle near him. However, he would be the first to break into a cheerful smile and laughter once the job was completed. He was a pride among friends and a true friend to all who knew him.

Strictly believed in productivity

Mansukh Bhai strictly believed in keeping his team members engaged and productive. He was always ready to provide additional tasks to those who finished their work early or were idle. He had a knack for finding new work for everyone daily, even those reluctant to work. He did all this with love and care, never harassing or causing unhappiness to any employee. One incident reflecting his overall team management approach would be worth noting.

One day, Mansukh Bhai was busy working in his office.

After completing the work, he handed over another task to his secretary. Meanwhile, while he was inspecting his office, he noticed that a senior employee working in the accounts section was sitting idle. He did not have any work. When Mansukh Bhai talked to that employee, he learned that the work he used to do was done quickly, so he used to sit idle till duty time was over. Mansukh Bhai heard this, thought for about two minutes, and then went to his cabin. After reaching the cabin, he called the employee and said, in straightforward words...

"Starting tomorrow, I would like you to work for me from 4 to 6 p.m.". The employee responded with a stutter, barely able to utter a word. "Your job will be to read the headlines of all the newspapers that come to the office every day and then note them down for me. Finally, I want you to narrate them to me," commanded Mansukh Bhai. The employee replied obediently, "Yes, Sir."

The employee was in a state of shock. He knew that he couldn't refuse the task assigned to him. However, he wondered if this could also be a job. But Mansukh Bhai always had more ideas brewing in his mind. He just waited for the right time to implement those ideas. As soon as he got the space, he started working on his new ideas and utilized the idle time of his employees. Later, describing this particular incident, Mansukh Bhai said that the order had two benefits: first, it provided an opportunity for the idle employee to learn something new, and second, it increased the employee's productivity. He was able to keep himself updated with the world's happenings through this employee, despite having limited chances to read newspapers. Mansukh Bhai's thinking shows that even though he was not highly educated and had no background in human resource management, he was skilled at giving new ideas to his employees for their development and taking productive work from them in their free time. In this way, he benefited himself and those who worked with him. He also realized the importance of information long ago and how having access to it could help a person do good for themselves, society, and the country.

Never indulged in cut-throat competition

Mansukh Bhai was a rare gem – a man of exceptional character and values, loved and respected by all who knew him. He had a gift for thoughtful and engaging conversation, and his friends never tired of discussing a wide range of topics with him - from business to social issues and new ideas. One of the things that made him so special was his ability to listen attentively and provide valuable advice to his friends while also being open to receiving advice from them in return. Despite being a person who rarely displayed his emotions, Mansukh Bhai was always respectful of the feelings of others. Even if he got angry with someone, he was quick to express his love and affection for them the next moment.

Mansukh Bhai's get-togethers with his friends usually extended well into the late evening, but he was always mindful of his work commitments. He knew when to leave early if needed, and he always maintained the quality of his work. For him, work was like worship, and he firmly believed in healthy competition in business. Unlike some of his peers, he maintained a cordial relationship with his competitors and never indulged in cut-throat competition. He promoted healthy competition and respected his rivals, always believing that everyone had the potential to succeed. Mansukh Bhai's strong friendships and approach to business had a lasting impact on everyone he met.

Never became a money-making machine

Mansukh Bhai was a man of great principles who believed in the value of hard work, sincerity, and relationships. He dedicated his entire life to achieving his goals without compromising his ethics. Despite his success, he never became a money-making machine and remained grounded throughout his journey. His kindness and generosity were renowned in the community. He lived to see five generations and left a legacy that future generations could easily carry forward. Mansukh Bhai deeply respected relationships and made sure to nurture them with utmost sincerity. He valued his family above all else and always prioritized their needs, even during the most challenging times. After a long day of work, Mansukh Bhai would come home and gather information about everyone, listen to their problems, and provide them with the needed support. He would spend his evenings fulfilling the needs of his loved ones and making sure they were happy and content.

18

Listen to Everyone, But Trust Your Own Instincts

"Critical thinking is the most important factor with chess. As it is in life, you need to think before you make decisions."

– Hikaru Nakamura, American Chess Grandmaster

Mansukh Bhai was a firm believer in the philosophy of life that while it is essential to consider the views and opinions of others, it is ultimately crucial to trust your instincts and do what feels right to you. Seeking advice and guidance from others can be helpful, but at the end of the day, you are the only one who truly knows yourself and should make decisions accordingly. So, listening to your inner voice and having faith in your abilities to make the right choices is essential.

He was a true master of listening and treating everyone with equal respect. But when it came to taking action, he followed his own instincts. He had an exceptional talent for linking his products with betterment of society and people's happiness, leaving no doubt that he was ahead of his time. His thought process was like a computer's, and he approached every matter in a highly calculated way, impressing those around him.

He was a moving organization...

Babuji was a moving organization and a person who valued establishing lifelong relationships with those he associated with. He instilled these same values in his children so that they could be useful to society and their country.

What stands out about Babuji is his unique approach towards trust. While most people tend to trust themselves, Babuji trusted his co-workers more than he trusted himself. He believed that the people who walked with him step by step were his wealth and that he had to trust them to move up the steps of progress. His story of Kuber is an incredible example of his faith in others, and it's something that anyone can learn from.

Inspirational stories of friendship...

During Diwali, Babuji played cards with friends as part of Shagun. No friend could dare to say no to card-playing. Babuji used to stay immersed in fun till midnight, playing cards and having fun with his friends. There are many stories of his deep relationships with friends, so sometimes it becomes difficult to believe in Babuji's personality. Even today, people remember those days. Babuji may have become rich, but he always maintained the qualities of humanity inherited from his parents. Once he learned about the illness of the rickshaw puller in whose rickshaw he often rode, he started keeping track of his well-being. He also helped as much as possible.

This tale of Babuji is a beacon of inspiration for us all. It underscores the significance of friendship, humanity, and kindness, even in the face of immense success. Despite his wealth and status,

Babuji always retained his humble beginnings and always made time for his friends. His love for playing cards and spending time with his loved ones brought immense joy and happiness to their lives. His dedication to the well-being of the rickshaw puller, even after achieving success, is a testament to his selflessness and genuine concern for others.

Maintained an excellent balance between family and work...

Here are lines from a famous poem by poet Om Vyas Om:

Pita jeevan hai, sambal hai , shakti hai,

Pita sristi ke nirman ki abhivyakti hai.

(Father is life, strength, power,

Father is the expression of creation)

These lines from Om Vyas Om's poem beautifully capture the essence of a father's role in our lives. They are the embodiment of life, strength, and power, and they play an integral role in the creation and development of our being. These words truly resonate with fathers' profound impact on our lives and underscore the importance of cherishing and honouring them.

Despite the heat of life's struggles, Mansukh Bhai became a well-rounded individual with an innate understanding of the philosophies of life. Even though he was always busy with work, he never let it hinder his love for his family. His kind and loving gestures infused enthusiasm among the children, and his affection towards people kept him connected with everyone.

In the early days, Mansukh Bhai and his family lived in a small one-room house on rent. Despite various challenges, such as power outages, Baa stayed up all night fanning the children with her hand to keep them cool. However, Mansukh Bhai was always prepared for such situations and would ensure that he had everything ready for the family in the morning.

Upon returning from work, Mansukh Bhai would often discuss business matters, but he would always take a moment to survey the house, ensuring everything was in order. Baa, understanding his priorities, knew that his thoughts were always on the family's well-being. Despite the numerous challenges they faced, Mansukh Bhai's unwavering dedication to his family was evident in his tireless efforts to provide them with a better life.

Mansukh Bhai's life was centred around his family, and he made a point to stay connected with his parents through regular letters. Upon receiving a letter, he would promptly reply, never forgetting to bring something sweet whenever he returned home. Furthermore, he would only sit down for dinner after spending quality time with the children, demonstrating his commitment to maintaining strong family bonds.

SCHOOL

19

Flag Bearer of Excellence in Education

"Knowledge is power. Information is liberating. Education is the premise of progress, in every society, in every family."

– Kofi Annan, Seventh Secretary-General of the United Nations

Mansukh Bhai's legacy is truly inspiring. Despite facing limited access to education, he firmly believed education was the key to unlocking a brighter future for the next generation. He spared no effort in pursuing high-quality education for all, opening multiple leading institutions to promote education in society. Decades ago, he recognized education's crucial role in personal and societal growth based on his own experiences. His dedication and vision have left an indelible mark on society, inspiring countless others to follow in his footsteps.

In his childhood, Mansukh Bhai often encountered the phrase Vidya Dadati Vinayam written at the entrance of schools. Curious about its meaning, he once asked his mother. She explained to him that education gives a person humility, which is necessary to understand the importance of conduct and behaviour. This knowledge is acquired through education, which makes a person humble. And this humility allows a person to do any work and earn wealth.

Despite having to abandon formal education at a young age, he held onto his mother's words of wisdom and lived a life filled with humility and hard work. He faced numerous challenges along his journey but persevered and eventually achieved financial success through dedication and determination. However, his success did not make him forget his roots. In fact, Mansukh Bhai decided to give back to society by arranging to educate as many children as possible. His kind heart and generosity knew no bounds as he wanted to ensure that these children would not have to endure the same struggles that he did.

Lack of education always troubled him emotionally

Despite his remarkable success, Mansukh Bhai always felt the emotional weight of not having completed formal education. Nevertheless, he persevered, often recalling a pivotal encounter from his past when he sold cigarettes on the bustling streets of Lucknow. During this time, he impressed a retired government official with his exceptional communication skills and sales prowess.

Once, that gentleman approached Mansukh Bhai and asked him about his earnings. "Brother, how much do you earn in this work?" he inquired. Why don't you do something else? You are good-looking, well-spoken, hardworking, and, most of all, you are amazingly punctual. I also find you very nice. Meet me tomorrow. I'll see what happens. Maybe something good will happen to you," the person added.

Mansukh Bhai replied politely, "Sir, I am not very educated. I don't even want to do a job now. I have done a lot of work. I am doing business. If people like you bless me, one day I will definitely become something."

The person then asked, "What is your age now? I will get you admission to the best institute in the city. If you are ready to study, then tell me. I think you can go far in your studies also. If you study, you will be more successful in business."

Mansukh Bhai's response was a polite smile and a gentle refusal. The situation was straightforward. Although he was of school age then, he was far from his studies. Education did play a role in his aspirations, but he had already made significant strides in business. His nature didn't allow him to turn back, so he politely declined the offer. However, he had already made up his mind to provide higher education to his children and future generations.

Had cherished the dream of compensating the deficiency...

Mansukh Bhai was a driven businessman, but he always retained sight of the power of education. He was determined to compensate for the lack of education in his own life and ensure that his children received the best education possible. He dreamed his children would achieve great things and set a new standard for future generations. He knew that education was vital for success in the future, and he instilled this belief in his children. His unwavering commitment to education paid off, and his children succeeded greatly. The power of education can truly make a difference in one's life, and Mansukh Bhai knew this better than anyone.

Though Mansukh Bhai was a busy businessman, his love for family was paramount. With his sharp acumen, he could see the future right before him. Meanwhile, Baa was busy imparting family values and providing a better upbringing for the children. She managed the household efficiently, so Mansukh Bhai could focus on his business. Baa played a dual role in the children's lives—that of a mother and a father. While the kids helped with household chores as they grew older, their studies remained a top priority. Mansukh Bhai clarified that their education should never be compromised, even if it meant cutting back on expenses. Thanks to Baa's hard work, the children excelled in their studies while contributing to the household. Mansukh Bhai was thrilled and expressed his gratitude to Baa for her dedication and efforts.

One day Mansukh Bhai said, "I think we should educate our children in Mumbai (then Bombay). They will not only study but will also learn the language and methods of business.... There are many businessmen there. Our children will learn something." Actually, Mansukh Bhai had decided that he would fulfill his dreams through children.

He said, "We will send the children to such good schools that the children will also be proud of, and the coming generations will also say that 'even though Mansukh Bhai could not study himself, he taught the children in the country's best schools'."

Struggle and a sense of social responsibility...

Mansukh Bhai, a man of great empathy and compassion, was deeply moved by the plight of underprivileged children. Even during his days of struggle, he couldn't bear the sight of young souls who were aimlessly wandering the streets, devoid of education. He often thought that if he had the financial means, he would open schools for all those children. His concern for the welfare of children extended to broader society, and he often found himself preoccupied with thoughts of how he could make a positive impact. Over time, this deep sense of social responsibility only grew stronger and more resolute within him, fuelling his determination to bring about a change, no matter the odds.

With Baa's consent, he sent his younger son, Deepak Bhai, to study at a renowned college in Mumbai. He firmly believed that education is the key to success and the most valuable asset that one can possess. He always said that the brain develops only through study and that education provides the ability to distinguish between right and wrong. Both of Mansukh Bhai's sons proved his belief in education right. They suggested new ways to take his business forward and brought innovation. As a result, many new startups were launched.

Always remembered his resolution

Babuji always remembered his resolution to contribute to society. He believed that education was crucial for the development of children, and he wanted to create educational institutions that would not only impart knowledge but also instill moral values and a sense of responsibility in the youth. He envisioned schools that would prepare children for higher education while teaching them traditional Indian knowledge. Babuji acquired land to build an educational institution, but unfortunately, his sons didn't show much interest in carrying forward his vision as they were equally busy with business commitments; Babuji felt disheartened and decided to talk to his son, Deepak, about it.

Mansukh Bhai, "Deepak, what happened to the school project on that plot in Noida…?"

Deepak Bhai: "Babuji, I haven't been able to start the work yet. I understand the urgency, and I will make it a priority." Mansukh Bhai was disappointed, and his following words pierced Deepak Bhai's conscience to the core.

Mansukh Bhai, "I hope the school will be opened before I breathe my last, right?"

Deepak Bhai was familiar with Babuji's unwavering determination. When asked about this matter, he quickly replied, 'Babuji… please don't say that… I will move as quickly as possible." Deepak Bhai wasted no time addressing Babuji's concerns and ensuring he was content. He even arranged to ensure that the school's foundation stone in Noida was immediately laid at the hands of Babuji. Following Babuji's' wishes, Deepak Bhai initiated a chain of Kothari International Schools nationwide. The first was established in Noida in 2006, then Mansukh Bhai National School in Pune in 2011, and the second Kothari International School in Pune in 2016. The year 2016 also marked the launch of a nationwide daycare chain for young children known as Kothari Starz. Thousands of children are provided with an excellent education in these modern facilities. *Mansukh Bhai always believed that education is the key to overall development and becoming a good person.*

He emphasized human values, humanity, family, society, and country more than money. Mansukh Bhai wanted children to follow those ideals in the interest of human beings, culture, and the nation. Therefore, he took up the responsibility of educating society. He could have run other businesses with the money he had spent building the school. He could have invested elsewhere, but he gave more importance to making children better humans than to money. All these schools represent the culmination of the visionary and arduous efforts of Mansukh Bhai. He always cherished the dream of nurturing the youth as an inspiration. He tried his best to make the children energetic, vibrant, dynamic, and capable of providing decisive leadership for the future in an inspiring environment. He believed it is the best introduction to family and values when children fulfill their responsibilities towards their parents, complete their unfinished tasks, and make their dreams come true.

A true pioneer of women's empowerment...

Women's empowerment was recognized as a central issue only after two and a half decades of the country's independence, but Babuji was ahead of his time in recognizing the importance of empowering women. He understood women's power and always gave proper respect to them. Throughout his life, he kept his wife Baa with him, sought her advice, and gave importance to her every word. Babuji's way of working involved making every female member of the family aware of the intricacies of the business, teaching them how to identify potential, and giving them knowledge about profit and loss. He even passed on his business tricks to his daughter-in-law, Arti Kothari, who runs the schools of their group very well with the help of her husband, Deepak Bhai. Arti Kothari credits her success to Babuji's blessings and encouragement, inspiring her even today. Babuji was a pioneer of women's empowerment, and his legacy lives on through the success of his family and their businesses.

The child within him came alive again

When Mansukh Bhai's dream of establishing schools finally came to fruition, it brought him a deep sense of satisfaction and flooded his mind with memories that made him truly happy. He made it a habit to visit both Kothari International School in Noida and Mansukh Bhai National School in Pune, positioning his chair by the window to watch the children play in the field. As he reminisced about his childhood in Narali village, he couldn't help but feel a tinge of sadness that his family's financial struggles prevented him from experiencing the same level of joy and carefree play. But now, having achieved so much in his life and reached a certain age, the childlike wonder within him was reborn. The sound of children's laughter and their games would fill him with immense happiness, and he would feel grateful to be able to contribute to their education and well-being.

20

No Beating a Retreat Attitude

"Big results require big ambitions."

– Heraclitus, Greek Philosopher

Mansukh Bhai's fearlessness and determination to break the shackles of poverty led him to leave home at a young age. He had no reservations about any work he pledged to do. He simply decided and started his journey, never looking back. Despite the difficulties encountered along the way, he remained undaunted and persevered. Although he waited until eighteen to take his first trip, his unwavering spirit and courage allowed him to overcome any obstacles he faced.

Babuji believed in living life to the fullest without considering it a burden. Despite his love for his village and its comfort, he chose to work in Kanpur from the beginning to earn a livelihood. Even though he missed the love and better food that he used to get from his mother in his village, he did not give up or become disheartened. He knew that the opportunities for growth and advancement were limited in the colonial village, so he controlled his emotions. Babuji believed that the nature of the work does not matter as much as our attitude towards it. He believed that when we start considering any work small or big, we start moulding ourselves accordingly, which can lead to problems.

Right from the beginning, Mansukh Bhai had the habit of multitasking. He dedicated himself to whatever work he did with complete honesty and commitment. His way of working showed that he was mindful of the future, but instead of worrying or dreaming about it, he lived in the present and focused on improving it. Despite facing adverse situations and struggling to make ends meet, he never let his circumstances become his weakness. He worked hard to complete his tasks quickly, which saved time and allowed him to look for other opportunities. As Babuji used to say, no matter how challenging the circumstances may be, absolute satisfaction lies in controlling them instead of being controlled by them.

While counting bricks, he learned about the work of hawking. This was a new opportunity for him when he lost his job. He observed the hawkers, their style, their way of working, and how they sold their goods. Then, he decided to pursue the hawking business. Despite all the privations, he was fully prepared mentally and physically to do it because he believed that—'It is during privations that the real test of physical and mental capacity takes place. When one is prosperous one can do anything. True character is tested only when your hands are empty and you try with all your might to fill them.' This shows that with the right mindset and attitude, one can overcome even the most difficult of circumstances.

Illumination of existence amidst destitution

The words of Pele, widely regarded as one of the greatest football players of all time, continue to inspire and motivate people worldwide. His quote, "Success is no accident. It is hard work, perseverance, learning, studying, sacrifice, and most of all, love of what you are doing or learning to do," is a reminder that success requires dedication, effort, and passion. Similarly, Mansukh Bhai's philosophy on success was equally powerful and straightforward. He believed one should never fear failure, especially when starting with nothing. It's essential to set goals and dream big, no matter how unattainable they may seem. Pursue your goals with honesty, dedication, and devotion, and keep pushing forward enthusiastically, even in the face of setbacks. When you achieve your goals, don't stop there. Set new ones and continue to challenge yourself. This is the essence of true success and the ultimate joy of life.

Babuji's thoughts about success centred on the idea that it can only be achieved through hard work and dedication. He believed that regardless of how far away one's goals may seem, anything can be accomplished with continuous effort. For Babuji, the true joy of success came from both the journey and the destination. When individuals are fully invested in their pursuits, they experience a deep sense of satisfaction that allows them to forget all their obstacles. This contentment and composure sets successful people apart from others, making them exceptional.

Mansukh Bhai's determination led him to climb the steps that eventually led him to his destination. Upon reaching there, he felt an overwhelming sense of happiness but didn't forget the moments he had spent contemplating. He didn't let his joy make him attached; instead, he became a bearer of the tradition of the great ascetics who followed the teachings of Lord Shri Krishna. One such teaching, *'Karmanyeva adhikar aste, ma phaleshu kadacha na'* from the Bhagavad Gita, part of the Mahabharata, resonated with him the most. This shloka means, "You have a right to perform your prescribed duty, but you are not entitled to the fruits of action." Mansukh Bhai followed this principle all his life and inspired many.

A humanist in the true sense...

William Shakespeare once said, "No legacy is so rich as honesty." This quote truly resonates with the legacy of Mansukh Bhai, a remarkable human being who embodied the values of honesty and generosity. He went above and beyond to ensure the well-being of his competitors, treating them not as adversaries but as fellow members of the business community. One touching incident from Mansukh Bhai's life exemplifies this spirit of compassion.

When Mansukh Bhai learned that a rival in the Pan Masala industry was experiencing difficulties, facing economic challenges and health issues, he immediately went to see him and offered his support. He gave him valuable health-related advice and wished him a speedy recovery, urging him to prioritize his health over his business worries. For Mansukh Bhai, good health was the foundation of a successful business. This aspect of his personality shows that he was a savvy businessman and a true humanist who cared deeply about his relationships.

21

An Amazing Spark – Working Even at 85

The vast ocean holds immense potential, but even the most experienced boatman can get tired. However, as long as there is a steady rhythm in his breath and the vibration of the waves, his hand will not falter.

–Anonymous

Mansukh Bhai must have been around eighty-five years of age at that time... While sitting in a wheelchair in his luxurious residence in Ahmedabad, he suddenly said to the servant of the house... "Please call Deepak...."

Saying "Yes... Yes..." the servant called his son Deepak...

Deepak Bhai, "Hello... *Bauji...*" (affectionately calling him *Bauji)*

Mansukh Bhai, "You come here, we have to discuss something important... quickly... quickly."

Deepak Bhai asked, "Bauji, is there something special...?"

Mansukh Bhai replied, "You come... then I will tell you."

Deepak Bhai was preoccupied with some other important work in Kanpur, but he knew that if Bauji had called, it must be something significant. Meanwhile, at home in Ahmedabad, Sharda Ben, Mansukh Bhai's wife, had no idea that her husband had contacted their son. Everything seemed normal at home, but Mansukh Bhai was preoccupied with his thoughts. He had a habit of maintaining friendships and good relationships with people, but he did not like the Panchayat on business principles. Deepak Bhai cancelled all his appointments in Kanpur and flew to Ahmedabad. It was morning when he arrived. Deepak Bhai looked at his father and found him okay, which relieved him. However, he felt that there must be something else going on. Meanwhile, Mansukh Bhai looked at his son Deepak, but he did not express his feelings or intentions immediately.

Deepak Bhai was worried as he anxiously asked his father, "Bauji, what is the matter?" However, Mansukh Bhai urged him to rest and have breakfast before discussing the matter. Deepak Bhai was surprised by his father's response but knew him well enough to realize he would never do anything if he didn't want to. As he went inside, his mother, Sharda Ben, was taken aback by his sudden appearance. "You! When did you come ?" she asked. Deepak Bhai explained that his father had called him. During lunch, Deepak Bhai once again inquired about the matter, but Mansukh Bhai remained silent. As lunch ended, Mansukh Bhai's mysterious behaviour left Deepak Bhai even more curious and eager to know more.

When the evening arrived, the family members gathered in the living room. Growing increasingly impatient, Deepak Bhai asked again, "Bauji, can you please tell me..." before being interrupted by Mansukh Bhai, who suggested that they all drink some tea first. The matter was again put on hold, much to Deepak Bhai's frustration. He continued to ponder over the issue but to no avail. Nothing out of the ordinary happened during dinner, and Sharda Ben wasn't particularly curious about the matter either. She knew that if Mansukh Bhai had called his son, it would probably have been regarding business, so she didn't show any interest.

After dinner, Mansukh Bhai called Deepak Bhai to his room…

Mansukh Bhai, "Deepak…."

Deepak Bhai, "Yes, 'Bauji'…."

Mansukh Bhai did not let any particular expression appear on his face… but with a slight smile, he said…

"Deepak…I am starting a new business of Pan Masala…"

Deepak Bhai was taken aback, but before he could respond, Mansukh Bhai continued with conviction, "Listen, I am about to launch a new brand, MMK. I believe in its potential. You join me as a partner…"

After Mansukh Bhai spoke, there was a moment of silence. Then, Deepak Bhai asked, "Bauji, are you saying that you want to start a new brand?"

"Yes, why not?" replied Babuji.

Deepak Bhai seemed hesitant and took a moment to respond. Eventually, he answered, but he did not give a clear response. Instead, he indirectly refused Bauji's idea.

Deepak Bhai's voice trembled with emotion as he spoke to Mansukh Bhai. "Bauji, what about Pan Parag? Isn't it yours? By competing with Pan Parag, you're going against yourself. Running MMK means ending Pan Parag's reign. If that's your goal, then so be it. But don't forget, just because you gave Pan Parag to me, doesn't mean your relationship with it has ended." Despite Deepak Bhai's passionate words, Mansukh Bhai remained composed, his gentle smile unwavering as he listened intently.

And when Deepak Bhai finally fell silent, Mansukh Bhai responded with equal calmness, saying, " Deepak, I find it difficult to spend my free time. All day long, I keep thinking about business and new ways to move forward. I agree that I have grown old... I can't walk alone, but for the sake of business, it is not necessary to physically move. My mind is not only walking but also racing. You know... I come up with at least two to four ideas for a new business daily. I feel like doing something new, but if you think that I am thinking unnecessarily or if you think that I want to spoil the established business, then this thinking needs to be corrected. If you want, there won't be any MMK... But think, how would it be if two pan masalas were from the same company group... We can capture the space left in the market as well. There are many local-level pan masalas available in the market. The brand name Pan Parag will be the strength behind MMK. The local ones will lose their share in the market if our price is low. But if you don't want this, then... leave..." Saying this, he stopped talking, which was like a signal to Deepak Bhai to leave. Deepak Bhai stood up before his father, went to Sharda Ben's room, and met everyone.

Deepak Bhai sought permission from his mother, Sharda Ben, and left Ahmedabad to return to Kanpur. Deepak Bhai couldn't help but reflect on Bauji's courage on his way back. He marvelled at how Babuji fearlessly pursued his dreams, achieving success with his business, Pan Parag, flying high. Despite reaching an age where most people would want to enjoy their life in peace, Bauji remained hungry for more, striving to reach new heights of fame and success. Deepak Bhai praised Bauji's unwavering courage and determination, acknowledging that he was an exceptional person.

Despite being eighty-five years old, his passion for innovation and new ideas was still as strong as ever. Though Deepak Bhai was mindful of his age and did not allow him to do as much as he wanted, Mansukh Bhai's sharp mind and innovative ideas were beyond compare. His wisdom and guidance could help anyone achieve success if they were willing to work hard and follow the right direction. Mansukh Bhai used to say, "If someone is willing to work day and night, then I can teach them the tricks of earning money because working hard in the right direction can make earning money easy."

Mansukh Bhai Mahadev Bhai Kothari was a true titan of entrepreneurship, and his contributions to the market, business, and startup worlds were nothing short of legendary. He established the revered traditions of Pan Parag, which earned him deep respect and admiration in Gujarati society. Kothari's unwavering dedication to the progress of others set him apart as a selfless leader, and his commitment to healthy competition instead of jealousy was a shining example to all. His inspiring thoughts, kind heart, and tireless work ethic remain a source of motivation for us to this day. His legacy reminds us that hard work, devotion, and perseverance are essential to achieving our goals and that nothing can stand in our way if we refuse to give up.

Mansukh Bhai, an extraordinary individual, was a true warrior on the path of karma. His unwavering commitment to his goals was a testament to his character. He was a passionate individual who valued success and was a beacon of friendship to all who knew him. His relationships were not just evergreen, but they were the very essence of his being. He lived life to the fullest, and even in moments of sorrow and pain, his infectious smile had the power to light up the darkest corners. Mansukh Bhai, a true *karmayogi,* embarked on his eternal journey on 27 November 2015, leaving behind a legacy that will forever be etched in our hearts.

His passing shocked many, and his loss was felt by his loved ones, colleagues, the FMCG community, and the millions of households that relied on his products. It was evident from the scenes of mourning in the streets of Kanpur, the crowds of mourners at Bhairav Ghat, and the sadness etched on the faces of those who knew him well. The ripple effect was felt throughout the pan masala industry, with associated sectors experiencing a period of stagnation. The tears shed by his relatives, friends, and employees served as a poignant reminder of the profound impact that one individual can have on the lives of so many.

The passing of Babuji has left a void, but his rich and glorious tradition lives on in the pages of golden history. His legacy of the incomparable Pan Parag continues to add sweetness to the lives of countless people - from family and friends to employees, distributors, and retailers. Even those who enjoy Pan Parag have been touched by his enduring legacy.

Babuji was a brilliant businessman and a caring and successful father who went to great lengths to provide his children with everything he never had. He always remembered his humble beginnings and remained committed to giving back to society, especially those standing at the ladder's last rung. Even in the last stage of his life, he kept business in mind, a testament to his unwavering dedication and passion for his work.

His absence is painful, but his remarkable legacy echoes: "It would have been even more fulfilling if you had been here. You would have witnessed that the seed you sowed has grown into a majestic banyan tree. Under its shade, every person who has ever connected with you is finding comfort. Though you're not physically present, we sense your presence. We are grateful for your unwavering inspiration and constant push towards our duties... we are grateful."

We will forever cherish his memory as a genuine *karmayogi,* our mentor and source of motivation. His brilliance will persistently guide us towards the path of righteousness and help us progress towards our goals every single day.

Baa's unbearable pain and those six months...

The pain and loss experienced by Baa after the passing of her beloved husband, Mansukh Bhai, was a profoundly poignant reminder that although she had always faced life's challenges with courage and strength, his absence left her utterly broken. She became quiet and withdrawn, and her eyes betrayed the unbearable pain she was feeling. Sadly, just six months later, on 4 May 2016, Baa also passed away, leaving behind a legacy of courage and resilience.

Legacy of unwavering focus on goals

The timeless tale of the *Mahabharata,* with its captivating narrative, holds a mirror to our modern lives, emphasizing the crucial role of unwavering focus. This quality, which immortalized Arjuna as the greatest archer of all time, is not just a relic of the past. In our contemporary world, time management experts have penned numerous works on the subject, echoing the sentiments of martial arts master Bruce Lee, who famously said, 'The successful warrior is the average man whose focus is like a laser.'

By reading the struggling journey of *karmapath* warrior Mansukh Bhai, today's young generation can develop the ability to focus on the goal. This is his most incredible legacy. Mansukh Bhai used to be serious about a goal like the bird's eye. He habitually contemplated his aspirations, carefully considering the best course of action. His passion burned brightly within him, fuelling his determination. With unwavering commitment, Mansukh Bhai was prepared to go to great lengths, overcoming any obstacle, in order to achieve his goal. Whatever Mansukh Bhai did, he did it with his whole heart, dedication, and mind—he lived it to the fullest. He was not satisfied even in happy moments.

Babuji's Entire Philosophy of Life in Quotations

1. Continuous action protects a person from bad habits, complaining, and boredom.
2. If one is dedicated to duty, courageous to struggle, and ready to work tirelessly, then such a person will achieve success.
3. Hard work, dedication, and punctuality are vital for business success.
4. Laughing all the time gives me new energy.
5. Talking to people and always learning something is crucial for success.
6. Don't make yourself sad by the success of the most successful person. Enjoy it. Try that like him, and you will reach the pinnacle of success. Learn the qualities of success from the most successful person.
7. Staying close to family increases love.
8. I find great joy in meeting people's needs. This is my achievement.
9. In India, with determination and continuous hard work, anyone can achieve financial abundance and become a millionaire.
10. I have a strong work ethic and enjoy being productive. By cultivating the habit of working diligently, tasks become more accessible and fulfilling.

11. I enjoy helping others by listening to their concerns and solving their problems.
12. I consider all my colleagues as valuable contributors to the success of our work. I am grateful for those who support and assist me along the way.
13. Fate plays a role in our lives, but we are also responsible for acting towards our goals.
14. Money is only valuable if it serves a greater purpose, such as helping others or promoting progress. The true power of wealth lies in its ability to empower the disadvantaged.
15. My life partner has been an unwavering source of support throughout my journey towards success.
16. Perseverance, dedication, and hard work are the keys to success.
17. Business decisions should be guided by rational principles rather than personal biases or external factors.
18. Upholding ethical principles is crucial in business. Conducting business with integrity is the foundation of long-term success.
19. My experiences and values can inspire others to pursue their dreams with determination and hard work.
20. To excel in any field, one must acquire the necessary skills and strive to perform at their best.
21. Time is a valuable resource, and those who manage it well are more likely to achieve their goals.
22. True achievement comes from hard work, not mere wishing or hoping for it to happen.
23. Once you step forward towards your goal, it's essential to keep moving forward and not look back.

24. Perseverance and determination are vital to completing any task you undertake, no matter what obstacles may come your way.
25. A keen sense of efficiency and good business acumen are essential to success in any venture.
26. Consistency and regularity are just as crucial as working quickly to achieve your goals.
27. Success is not easy, but those willing to work tirelessly and learn from others will eventually achieve it.
28. Life is too short to dwell on sadness, so it is essential to try to find happiness wherever possible.
29. Love and kindness can overcome even the most profound sadness.
30. Proper time management is crucial for success in both personal and professional life.
31. To be successful, you must have a strong morale, unwavering determination, and an unrelenting work ethic.
32. Success results from hard work, persistence, and a willingness to learn from mistakes.
33. Laziness is a waste of time, and time is our most valuable resource.
34. A good salesman possesses honesty, reliability, and the ability to connect with customers on a personal level.
35. Strength is not measured by anger or aggression but by remaining calm and level-headed in difficult situations.
36. Doing wrong to others is never the answer, as karma has a way of evening things out.

37. Arrogance is a toxic trait that can spread quickly if left unchecked, so it is essential to remain humble and grounded in all you do.

38. *Sarve bhavantu sukhina* is my dream. All should be happy, free from diseases, and witness auspicious events, and no one should have to become a part of sorrow.

AN IMPACT FEATURE

PAN INDIAN

Superior product design, impeccable quality, easy availability, pricing and publicity are the five factors that have made Pan Parag the leader in the pan masala market

"Pan masala *matlab* Pan Parag." "For us in Mumbai, Pan Parag pouches are as good as currency." "Wherever you find an Indian, you will find Pan Parag." These are just some of the reactions we got from people who were asked to comment on what Pan Parag meant to them. Not surprising when you consider that Kothari Products Limited (KPL) manufactures 100 sachets of Pan Parag every second, and the name has virtually become generic for mouth fresheners.

The company began small. Kothari Products was started by Mansukhbhai Mahadevbhai Kothari (affectionately known as MMK), a trader who shifted from Gujarat to Kanpur in 1942 to earn his livelihood. Before 1973, pan masala was available only in loose form. MMK decided to set up a factory for the production of pan masala and to market it under the Pan Parag brand name.

M.M. KOTHARI (MMK)
Chairman Pan Parag

It was MMK who decided to set up a factory for the production of pan masala and to sell it under a brand name.

"The idea was born when I saw people waiting for pan to be prepared for them at pan shops. I wanted to deliver something that they could carry with ease and savour as and when they wanted. I started my business on August 18, 1973 with just Rs 12,000 and personally handled all aspects of the business," remembers MMK. "Ours was the first branded product in the category and we had to create huge customer awareness to sell the product. There were many who had doubts over our business idea and the model."

Typically, pan masala is a simple mixture of betel nut, cardamom, lime and catechu and has a spray of natural perfumes. The Kotharis developed a secret formula for their product with a freshening flavour. By the mid-1980s, the Pan Parag brand was well established. "In June 1985, I decided to sell Pan Parag in pouches in an effort to expand the customer base," recalls Deepak Kothari, managing director of Kothari Products. Accordingly, the company imported a pouch-making machine. The machine worked wonders and turned the brand into a gold mine for the Kotharis. Today, Pan Parag is a household name.

According to MMK, it is the "self reliance" of Kothari Products which sets it apart from its competitors. "We are the only company that has never taken any credit from a bank or a financial institution. Besides, we have always had an eye on the future. We were the first player to recognise cricket as a major advertising opportunity and bought score strips on Doordarshan for as little as Rs 10,000 a match. Today we are the principal sponsors of the Pan Parag Zee Cine Awards, hitherto the domain of multinationals," he says.

Superior product design, quality, availability, pricing and publicity are the five guiding principles that Deepak Kothari and his company live by. He says it is this five-point charter that gives the tobacco-free Pan Parag an 80 per cent share of the market.

The Kotharis have now diversified into other businesses too. Deepak now mainly handles the family's new products, real estate and housing interests while his son Mitesh looks after Pan Parag's marketing and factories. Mitesh, who received his higher education in the UK, is the new face of the Kothari empire and enjoys the full confidence of his father and grandfather MMK.

My mother is behind the success of our company

Deepak Kothari, the managing director of KPL, is setting new goals for himself. Having raced much ahead of his competitors in the pan masala segment, he hates any complacency and is determined to stay at the top.

Q: How do you feel about being at the top of the market in the pan masala segment?

A: While Pan Parag is undoubtedly the leader of the pan masala market, I cannot say that I am satisfied with our position. I would hate to be complacent about where my company stands today. There are some players who are racing close behind. This is a good development for the market though. The 1980s were a golden period for us as we were the only major player in this segment. Now we are expanding our base to foreign countries. Already in the Middle East and Pakistan, Pan Parag has penetrated deep into the market and there is no one to compete with us out there.

Q: What would you cite as the reason for your product's phenomenal success?

A: If I had to name any one thing that changed the fortune of our company overnight, I would have to cite the launch of Pan Parag in sachets. Till June 1985, Pan Parag was available only in tin boxes, which were affordable only to a select category of purchasers. We wanted to popularise it even among rickshaw-pullers, and therefore imported a sachet making machine. Soon, Pan Parag was selling like hot cakes and a new base of customers was created. And I am happy to say that this category is still growing.

Q: Who would you attribute Pan Parag's success to?

A: Though my father M.M. Kothari was in the forefront, it was my mother Sharda Kothari, who was the key to our success. She is the sort of person who is always goading everyone in the family to work harder. If somebody is down with fever, she will immediately come with medicines and then say, 'Now go to work'. She is the woman behind our success. A hardworking and god-fearing woman, she takes care of all the employees of the company like a mother. It is she who has turned us into high achievers.

Q: What are the new business plans of the company?

A: While I would not like to disclose details, I can tell you that we are going to launch more consumer items soon. We have already diversified into real estate and housing in Maharashtra and Gujarat. The housing sector offers immense potential. Here too, we will work on the same pattern as Pan Parag. The motto of the company in the housing sector will be to ensure availability for the upper segments of society as well as for the poor.

Q: Has the ban on pan masala compelled you to enter other sectors?

A: We had already diversified into other consumer products. But I would like to strongly condemn the government's discriminatory policy. If it is banning pan masala because it is harmful, it should also ban tobacco products and cigarette. Why single out pan masala as a health hazard, when it is just a mouth freshener? Anything taken in excess is bound to create health problems, even a rasgulla or milk.

Q: There are reports that you are shifting your establishment out of Kanpur. Is that true?

A: I am sad to say that it is true. The state no longer offers good infrastructure facilities or an atmosphere where industry can flourish. So we have shifted our base to Gujarat and the North-east. However, our business association and bonds with Kanpur will always remain.

धूम मचा दे... रंग जमा दे,
हर दिल को दिवाना बना दे।
पान पराग
पान पराग
पान मसाला
कोठारी केमिकल्स, २६/५० बिरहाना रोड, कानपुर.

PAN PARAG
DELICIOUS
PAN KA MASALA

प्यारा सा स्वाद
जोड़े सबको साथ
पान पराग
पान मसाला

ड्रीमगर्ल की पसंद सेवन अप
हेमा मालिनी
सेवन अप
नारियल तेल
बूँद बूँद बिल्कुल शुद्ध!
कोठारी उत्पादन

धूम मचा दे... रंग जमा दे
PAN PARAG
पान पराग
लाखों की पसन्द
पान पराग
पान मसाला

धूम मचा दे...
रंग जमा दे
PAN PARAG
DELICIOUS
पान पराग
पान मसाला
दुनियाँ में सबसे ज़्यादा बिकनेवाला

प्यारा सा स्वाद
बाँधे सबको साथ
पान पराग
पान मसाला
धूम मचा दे... रंग जमा दे
प्यारा सा स्वाद
बाँधे सबको साथ
पान पराग
पान मसाला
धूम मचा दे... रंग जमा दे

चम-चमाचम...बजट आया !
BUDGET
बजट
वाशिंग पाउडर

सफ़ेदी का पैग़ाम
बजट
बजट
बजट

पान पराग
स्वादिष्ट
पान मसाला

धूम मचा दे...
रंग जमा दे.
पान पराग
पान मसाला एवं गुटखा

पान पराग
स्वादिष्ट
पान मसाला

मस्ती का आलम !
पान पराग

धूम मचा दे... रंग जमा दे.
आपका मनपसंद पान पराग,
डिब्बे और सुविधाजनक पाउच में.
पान पराग
पान मसाला
कोठारी उत्पादन